"This is a much needed book
tarian and what are the implic:
ships. This is a robust conversation among leading Southern Baptist
theologians on whether there is any eternal submission/subordination
between the divine persons and to what extent husband and wife are
an analogy for trinitarian relations. A must read for anyone interested
in trinitarian theology and what it means to call a doctrine 'biblical.'"
—**Mike Bird**, academic dean and lecturer in theology, Ridley College

"This little volume offers readers a window into an important ongoing
conversation in evangelical life about the doctrine of the Trinity and
its implications for human relationships and gender debates. Here,
readers will find helpful insights from exegesis, tradition, and theological method, as well as a healthy, God-honoring model for navigating
our theological disagreements. Highly recommended."
—**Rhyne Putman**, associate professor of theology and
culture, New Orleans Baptist Theological Seminary

"The doctrine of the Trinity has gained a position of prominence
in evangelical theology over the past few years largely due to (often
heated) debates surrounding the eternal relations of the Father and
the Son. While debates are rarely pleasant, they are often necessary,
especially when doctrines of supreme importance are at stake. The
present volume contains clear and up to date chapters by Bruce Ware,
Malcolm Yarnell, Matthew Emerson, and Luke Stamps that represent
various views of the Trinity held among Southern Baptist theologians
today, along with an introduction and conclusion by Keith Whitfield
that ably maps the issues at stake. With discussions marked by charity,
as well as incisive analysis and critique, contributors debate issues such
as the eternal functional subordination of the Son, the nature of the
God-human relationship, and theological method, making this volume useful for a broad evangelical readership. My prayer is that it will
serve not only Southern Baptists but also all confessional Protestants in
retrieving and renewing our confession of faith in the blessed Trinity,
who alone is worthy of our praise."
—**Scott Swain**, president and James Woodrow Hassell Professor
of Systematic Theology, Reformed Theological Seminary

TRINITARIAN
THEOLOGY

*Theological Models
and Doctrinal Application*

TRINITARIAN
THEOLOGY

*Theological Models
and Doctrinal Application*

Contributors:
BRUCE WARE, MALCOLM B. YARNELL III,
MATTHEW Y. EMERSON, and LUKE STAMPS

Editor: KEITH S. WHITFIELD

ACADEMIC
NASHVILLE, TENNESSEE

To our friend Steve McKinion and his family,
who, before this project started,
and while the project was being worked on,
have been kept by our triune God
and
have cast their faith consistently on him.

TABLE OF CONTENTS

Introduction

BY KEITH S. WHITFIELD

At the 2014 Southern Baptist Convention (SBC), a small group of professors from SBC seminaries and universities ate dinner together at La Tavola in Baltimore, Maryland. Over the course of the meal, we envisioned starting a fellowship for SBC professors to provide an opportunity to network across Southern Baptist institutions, to promote the role of the professor in Southern Baptist life, and to encourage scholarship in the churches of the SBC.

As I write this introduction of *Trinitarian Theology: Theological Models and Doctrinal Application*, the Southern Baptist Professor Fellowship has met annually in San Diego, Atlanta, San Antonio, and Providence during the annual meeting of the Evangelical Theological Society. The Fellowship has also hosted a couple of small topical events. At the 2015 Atlanta meeting, we held a small breakfast event at which Bruce Ware, Steve McKinion, and Malcolm Yarnell were invited to discuss appropriate methods for forming the doctrine of the Trinity and implications for applying trinitarian doctrine to complementarianism. We considered the proper application of Augustine's partitive exegesis and trinitarian reading of Scripture. Panelists interpreted both John 8:42 and 1 Cor 15:28 as they addressed the Son's relationship to the Father with respect to divine works in the immanent and economic Trinity. Finally, we asked whether there are certain boundaries that should be observed when applying trinitarian theology to the realm of human life and relationships. This book is a product of that conversation. Matthew Emerson and Luke Stamps contributed to this book in the place of Steve McKinion, who needed to step away from the project to care for his family during his youngest son's leukemia treatment.

Contemporary Trinitarian Debates within Evangelicalism

While the interactions in this book are between Southern Baptist theologians, the occasion for this book is situated within Evangelical concerns over trinitarian theology. In recent years, debates over trinitarian doctrine have emerged within evangelicalism. Three features of this doctrine have been central to these discussions. One of those points of discussion relates to whether the classical (or Latin) and social (or Eastern)[1] conceptions of the Trinity are both appropriate biblical models for conceptualizing the Trinity.[2] The difference between the classical and social models has been examined in

---

[1] See John Thompson, *Modern Trinitarian Perspective* (New York: Oxford University Press, 1994), 143–49. The label social Trinity seems to be first used by Jürgen Moltmann, *The Trinity and the Kingdom of God* (London: SCM, 1981), 157. Cornelius Plantinga has become well known by his affirmation of this model. See his "Social Trinity and Tritheism," in *Trinity, Incarnation and Atonement: Philosophical and Theological Essays*, ed. Ronald J. Feenstra and Cornelius Plantinga Jr. (Notre Dame, IN: University of Notre Dame Press, 1990).

[2] Cf. J. Scott Horrell, "Toward a Biblical Model of Social Trinity: Avoiding Equivocation of Nature and Order," *JETS* 47 (2004): 399–421; and Mark Husbands, "The Trinity Is *Not* Our Social Program: Volf, Gregory of Nyssa and Barth," in *Trinitarian Theology for the Church: Scripture, Community, Worship*, ed.

modern theology, but the renewed interest in trinitarian theology and the influence of the contemporary applications of these models situated the importance of this topic in evangelicalism. The church affirmed that God has one substance (*ousia*) and eternally and fully exists as three distinct persons (*hypostases* in Greek, *personae* in Latin). But exactly how one should understand the relationship between the substantial unity and personal plurality of the Godhead has been a point of theological debate. The classical and social models differ in large part based on where one starts in formulating their trinitarian doctrine and the emphasis one places on aspects of their conception. The classical model prioritizes the unity of the persons, because they share the divine essence and divine operations. This model seeks to demonstrate how one divine essence can exist in three distinct persons. The social model, which some claim follows the Cappadocians, starts with the analogy of persons in relation and affirming that the divine hypostases are fully personal in the modern sense of the term, emphasizing persons as having distinct personalities.[3] The social trinitarian model faces the challenge of explaining how the three persons in these terms are in fact one.[4]

The next trinitarian debate pertains to the doctrine of "Eternal generation." Athanasius used the phrase to communicate the Son's

---

Daniel J. Treier and David Lauber (Downers Grove, IL: InterVarsity, 2009), 120–41.

[3] Stephen Holmes challenges this understanding in *The Quest for the Trinity*. He argues that the East and West "essentially spoke with one voice." See Stephen R. Holmes, *The Quest for the Trinity* (Downers Grove, IL: InterVarsity, 2012), 144, cf. 129–31.

[4] In his assessment of trinitarian resurgence in evangelicalism, Jason Sexton points out social trinitarianism has been affirmed by prominent evangelical theologians. Yet prominence of social trinitarianism in evangelicalism is no longer what it has been. He notes many have been sharply critical of this approach, and Stanley Grenz moved away from the model later in his life. See "The State of Evangelical Trinitarian Resurgence," *JETS* 54 (2011): 791–93.

oneness with the Father. The doctrine is expressed in the Nicene Creed
in the phrases "begotten of the Father" and "light of light." Stephen
Holmes and others argue that "eternal generation" is an essential feature of orthodox trinitarian formulation, because the doctrine is central to the doctrine of the Trinity, soteriology, and God's purpose for
revealing himself.[5] Many evangelicals, however, have not affirmed the
doctrine of eternal generation, and have questioned its significance
for trinitarian theology and Christology.[6] In recent years, there has
been some movement toward a consensus on affirming the doctrine
of eternal generation. Yet, not everyone affirming this doctrine is clear
on what it means or why it is important.

The final evangelical trinitarian debate considers whether eternal
functional subordination (EFS) is the proper theological category for
conceiving the eternal relationship between divine persons in the triune life. EFS affirms that the divine persons are ontologically equal and
one, but, at the same time, the Son and the Spirit are subordinate to
the Father eternally and functionally. Throughout 2015–2016, this discussion received renewed interest in response to the publication of *One
God in Three Persons* edited by Bruce Ware and John Starke.[7] Specifically,
in June 2016, Liam Goligher and Carl Trueman challenged the claim
that the Son and the Spirit are subordinate to the Father eternally in

---

[5] Holmes, *Quest for the Trinity*, 87. See also Kevin Giles, *The Eternal Generation
of the Son: Maintaining Orthodoxy in Trinitarian Theology* (Downers Grove, IL:
InterVarsity, 2012); and Fred Sanders and Scott R. Swain, eds., *Retrieving Eternal
Generation* (Grand Rapids: Zondervan, 2017).

[6] See Millard Erickson, *Who's Tampering with the Trinity? An Assessment of the
Subordination Debate* (Grand Rapids: Kregel Academic, 2009); John S. Feinberg,
No One like Him: The Doctrine of God (Wheaton, IL: Crossway, 2001); Wayne
Grudem, *Systematic Theology* (Grand Rapids: Zondervan, 1994); and Bruce A.
Ware, *Father, Son, and Holy Spirit: Relationships, Roles, and Relevance* (Wheaton, IL:
Crossway, 2005).

[7] Bruce A. Ware and John Starke, eds., *One God in Three Persons: Unity of
Essence, Distinction of Persons, Implications for Life* (Wheaton, IL: Crossway, 2015).

terms of their divine functions. The debate was vigorously discussed throughout the summer, with more than 200 blog posts published on the topic in a little more than two months. Evangelical theologians such as Bruce Ware, Wayne Grudem, Denny Burk, Mark Thompson, and Mike Ovey have affirmed some articulation of the EFS position. Evangelical theologians such as Liam Goligher, Carl Trueman, Darren Sumner, Mark Jones, Scot McKnight, Matt Emerson, Luke Stamps, Scott Swain, and Fred Sanders believe that EFS represents a move away from traditional Christian orthodoxy.

There are at least five critical questions in this debate. First, is EFS of the Son and the Spirit to the Father taught in Scripture? The Bible indicates that the Son submits to the Father while he is incarnated (John 5:19), and this submission seems to continue into the future, at least in some sense (1 Cor 15:27–28). This position also teaches that the Son has been submissive to the Father from eternity. The biblical question is, what is meant by the Father "sending" the Son (John 3:17; 1 John 4:14) and by the Father being the "head" of Christ (1 Cor 11:3)? Is eternal functional subordination entailed in the very language of Father and Son?

Second, is the EFS of the Son an innovative theological position? Perhaps another way to ask the question is, was EFS affirmed by the early expositions of trinitarian doctrine? Wayne Grudem has argued that EFS has been consistently taught, and he provides extensive citations of how it has been affirmed throughout the history of the church.[8] Many others have argued that the church did not teach EFS, and would not have affirmed it as a way to conceive of the eternal relationships between the Father and the Son. They argue instead that historically the divine *taxis* properly reveal the relations and the

---

[8] Wayne Grudem, "Whose Position on the Trinity Is Really New?" The Council on Biblical Manhood and Womanhood, June 9, 2016, accessed March 6, 2018, https://cbmw.org/public-square/whose-position-on-the-trinity-is-really-new/.

distinctions between the divine persons. Further, they argue that the divine names reveal the *taxis*, but do not entail EFS.[9]

The third question raised by this debate is, if you affirm EFS, does that entail affirming a separation of the divine will? Many who affirm the classical trinitarian doctrine argue that the claim that the Son eternally submits to the Father implies two wills in God.[10] For the Son to

---

[9] Fred Sanders, *The Triune God* (Grand Rapids: Zondervan, 2016), 121–53, 200–04; Donald Fairbairn, *Life in the Trinity: An Introduction to Theology with the Help of the Church Fathers* (Downers Grove, IL: InterVarsity, 2009), 13–84; Richard Bauckham, "The Trinity and the Gospel of John," in *The Essential Trinity*, ed. Brandon D. Crowe and Carl R. Trueman (Phillipsburg, NJ: P&R, 2017), 83–106; Gilles Emery, *The Trinity: An Introduction to Catholic Doctrine on the Triune God* (Washington, DC: Catholic University of America Press, 2011), 111–58; Holmes, *Quest for the Trinity*, 53–55; R. Kendall Soulen, *The Divine Names and the Holy Trinity, Volume One: Distinguishing the Voices* (Louisville, KY: Westminster/John Knox, 2011); and Scott Swain, "Divine Trinity," in *Christian Dogmatics: Reformed Theology for the Church Catholic*, ed. Michael Allen and Scott Swain (Grand Rapids: Baker Academic, 2016), 78–106.

[10] D. Glenn Butner Jr., "Eternal Functional Subordination and the Problem of the Divine Will," *ETS* 58, no. 1 (2015): 131–49; Thomas H. McCall, *Which Trinity? Whose Monotheism? Philosophical and Systematic Theologians on the Metaphysics of Trinitarian Theology* (Grand Rapids: Eerdmans, 2010), 178–79; Millard Erickson, *Who's Tampering with the Trinity? An Assessment of the Subordination Debate* (Grand Rapids: Kregel, 2009), 172; Gilbert Bilezikian, "Hermeneutical Bungee-Jumping: Subordination in the Godhead," *JETS* 40, no. 1 (March 1997): 64; Steven Holmes, "Reflection on a New Defence of 'Complementarianism,'" *Shored Fragments* (blog), May 22, 2015, accessed April 25, 2018, http://steverholmes.org.uk/blog/?p=7507; Alastair Roberts, "The Eternal Subordination of the Son, Social Trinitarianism, and Ectypal Theology," *Alastair's Adversaria* (blog), May 31, 2015, accessed April 25, 2018, https://alastairadversaria.com/2015/05/31/the-eternal-subordination-of-the-son-social-trinitarianism-and-ectypal-theology/; Kevin DeYoung, "Distinguishing among the Three Persons of the Trinity within the Reformed Tradition," *DeYoung, Restless, and Reformed* (blog), The Gospel Coalition, September 27, 2016, accessed April 25, 2018, https://www.thegospelcoalition.org/blogs/kevin-deyoung/distinguishing-among-the-three-persons-of-the-trinity-within-the-reformed-tradition/; and Matthew Barrett, "Meet My Good Friend John Owen: One Will, Distinct Acts, and the Covenant of Redemption," *Credo*, June 21, 2016, accessed April 25,

submit to the Father's authority, there must be a distinction between the will of the Father and the will of the Son. Because will has historically been a property of nature and not person, affirming a separation in the divine wills is theologically problematic. To affirm a distinction between the Father's will and the Son's will after the incarnation is acceptable, but before the incarnation, it means God has two wills and implies a denial of divine simplicity.

The fourth question leads us back to the second terrain we crossed relating to evangelical trinitarian debate. Does the EFS of the Son deny the doctrine of eternal generation of the Son? As previously mentioned, this doctrine has been denied in recent years by evangelicals for various reasons. Their theological judgments on this doctrine have been based largely on certain hermeneutical and methodological convictions and questions about what the doctrine of eternal generation means. For those who affirm what some call the "classical" view of the Trinity, eternal generation is an important doctrine that expresses the unique relationship between the Father and the Son, as eternal procession expresses the unique relationship between the Father and the Spirit. Eternal generation for them does not conceive of a hierarchy in the Godhead. It communicates relationship of origin. Eternal generation conceptualizes relationship of distinction.[11]

Finally, should the relationships between the Father and Son be used to ground and explain the roles between men and women? The relevance of the Trinity as a theological basis for the complementary male-female relationships in the home, church, and broader societal domains has been a point of debate within evangelicalism for some

---

2018, http://credomag.com/2016/06/21/meet-my-good-friend-john-owen -one-will-distinct-acts-and-the-covenant-of-redemption-matthew-barrett/.

[11] Bruce Ware, "God the Son—At Once Eternally God with His Father, and Eternally Son of the Father," *Reformation21* (blog), Alliance of Confessing Evangelicals, June 9, 2016, accessed March 6, 2018, http://www.reformation21.org /blog/2016/06/god-the-sonat-once-eternally-g.php; Grudem, "Whose Position on the Trinity Is Really New?"

time. While this question no doubt relates to some exegetical considerations around texts like 1 Cor 11:3, the question is more directly about
how the analogy of being informs one's theological method.

Southern Baptists and Trinitarian Theology

Early in the dustup over the publication of *One God in Three Persons*,
on his blog, Michael Bird raised the ire of SBC theologians when he
wrote, "Given the centrality of this school of thought around Wayne
Grudem and Bruce Ware, I propose—for discussion—whether it is apt
to start referring to 'Southern Baptist Homoianism.'"[12] After suggesting the use of this theological reference for Southern Baptist theologians, he added, "Comments for and against appreciated!"[13] This
project is not a 60,000-word comment "for" or "against" a blog post. It

---

[12] Homoian trinitarian theology arises in the late fourth and fifth centuries, after the death of Arius. Concerned about the modalistic inclinations of
Sabellianism and, in their judgment, lack of biblical evidence for *homoousion*,
the homoians taught that the Son was like the Father, but not equal to the
Father in divine essence.

[13] Michael F. Bird, "Trinity Book Fest—Part 3: One God in Three Persons,"
Euangelion (blog), Patheos Evangelical, August 10, 2015, accessed March 6, 2018,
http://www.patheos.com/blogs/euangelion/2015/08/trinity-book-fest-part-3
-one-god-in-three-persons/. On subsequent reflection, Bird has communicated
[by email] that he sees some analogies between Ware and Grudem and the
ancient heresy of Homoianism, i.e., their focus on economic relationships,
their penchant for subordination and submission, their - until recently - ambiv-
alence about eternal subordination, and their championing of the language
of the Father's supremacy, all of this reminds Bird of the Homoians. However,
to be fair to Ware and Grudem, Bird does not consider them purely a rehash
Homoianism because they do not think Jesus is like the Father nor do they
consider the Son the Father's creature. Bird's stated concern is that ERAS/EFS
does resemble, in some respects but not all, Homoianism. Homoian trinitarian
theology arises in the late fourth and fifth centuries, after the death of Arius.
Concerned about the modalistic inclinations of Sabellianism and, in their judgment, lack of biblical evidence for *homoousion*, the homoians taught that the Son
was like the Father, but not equal to the Father in divine essence.

is, however, a response to a question Bird's comment, perhaps unintentionally, raises. Is there a consensus among Southern Baptists on the method of formulating trinitarian doctrine and how that doctrine may be applied to human relationships?

One might suppose that Southern Baptist confessional documents would supply a sufficient starting place to answer this question. We do find in these documents that some Southern Baptist confessions have in fact lacked the precise trinitarian language that reflects trinitarian orthodoxy. The problem implicit in these statements, however, does not suggest any form of subordination. Rather, some of the documents did not explicitly affirm the reality of distinct triune persons. Thus, Douglas Blount suggests that the 1925 and 1963 editions of the Baptist Faith and Message "fail to affirm unequivocally the Baptist commitment to God's triunity,"[14] opening the possibility for someone to affirm the statement and yet deny that God subsists as three persons. In the 1963 edition, the article reads: "[T]he eternal God reveals Himself to us as Father, Son, and Holy Spirit, each with distinct personal attributes, but without division of nature, essence, or being."[15] This language was appropriated from the Abstract of Principles, and represents a less precise doctrine compared to the trinitarian statement found in the New Hampshire Confession, on which the drafters of the 1925 Baptist Faith and Message (BF&M) relied heavily. New Hampshire's article on the Trinity represents more clearly trinitarian orthodox: "That there is one, and only one, living and true God . . . revealed under the personal and relative distinctions of the Father, the

---

[14] Douglas K. Blount, "Article II: God," in *The Baptist Faith and Message 2000: Critical Issues in America's Largest Protestant Denomination*, ed. Douglas K. Blount and Joseph D. Wooddell (New York: Rowman & Littlefield, 2007), 18.

[15] In the text, we cite the relevant sentence from the 1963 Baptist Faith and Message. Minor differences exist in the language of the 1925 and 1963 editions on this point. The 1925 reads: "He is revealed to us as Father, Son, and Holy Spirit, each with distinct personal attributes, but without division of nature, essence, or being."

Son, and the Holy Spirit; equal in every divine perfection, and executing distinct but harmonious offices in the great work of redemption."[16] In 2000, the committee that revised the BF&M removed the potential problem by adding the word "triune," so that it now reads, "The eternal *triune* [italics added] God reveals Himself to us as Father, Son, and Holy Spirit, each with distinct personal attributes, but without division of nature, essence, or being."

Southern Baptists cooperate under broad confessional commitments. We are not theologically uniform. Throughout our history, theological differences and debate within the SBC has been common. We have engaged in theological refinement at meetings of local Baptist associations, in Baptist state papers, and from both the pulpit and the floor of the annual meeting of the Southern Baptist Convention. We continue to debate our theological disagreements to clarify our statements, not for the simple delight in nuance, but because we believe theology matters for the health of local congregations, the witness to Christ in our communities, and the cooperative work of Southern Baptist churches. We want all confessing Southern Baptists to have a deeply formed faith. We want strong churches that teach and live "the faith that was delivered to the saints once for all" (Jude 3 CSB). Theological discussions help us think clearly about our faith as we seek the best way to conceptualize and articulate what we believe, so that the church can flourish in living her faith around the world with a clear and compelling witness to Christ. We believe that our theological conversations, done well, can facilitate meaningful cooperation. While our theological differences within the bounds of the BF&M are not insignificant, they should not divide us or restrain our partnership to magnify Christ and expand his kingdom. In this book, trinitariansim is discussed by Southern Baptists differently within the bounds of the BF&M.

---

[16] Williams L. Lumpkin, *Baptist Confessions of Faith* (Valley Forge, PA: Judson, 1969), 362.

In the first chapter, Bruce Ware claims that the nomenclature "Father, Son, and Holy Spirit" reveals a prevailing authority-submission structure within the Trinity. He describes his view as "eternal relations of authority and submission" (ERAS) and establishes a preference for that description over "eternal functional subordination" (EFS). He argues that conceiving the eternal relationship between Father and Son need not compromise the eternal unity or equality of the Godhead. The functional distinctions aid us in conceptualizing the threeness of God without compromising God's essential unity. In chapter 4, Ware responds to Yarnell's and Emerson and Stamps's chapters by affirming places of agreement in terms of trinitarian doctrine and key methodological commitments. He also illuminates where he differs with Emerson and Stamps's critique of ERAS. Throughout this interaction, Ware establishes additional support for his position in light of the concerns expressed by Emerson and Stamps in their chapter.

In the second chapter, Yarnell offers a trinitarian method for theological anthropology. He explores the proper relationship between anthropology and theology proper, the perspicuity of divine revelation, and the nature of the triune God revealed in divine names "Father, Son, and Holy Spirit." Yarnell's theological anthropology is based on humanity being created in the image of God. He argues that there are sound reasons to think that the relations within God provide a pattern for human relations, including male and female relations. In his responses to Ware, and Emerson and Stamps in the fifth chapter, he raises methodological concerns with correlating too closely our anthropological claims with our doctrine of God. Thus, he raises reservations regarding the concept of an eternal relation of authority and submission in the Trinity. While Yarnell commends Emerson and Stamps's "holistic theological method" and "thick biblicism," he states that his method is less reliant on tradition. Nevertheless, a significant portion of his response chapter depends on a theological reading of Scripture with the tradition.

In the third chapter, Matthew Emerson and Luke Stamps propose a method for determining whether a doctrine is biblical. Their
method entails interpreting Scripture canonically, confessionally, and
dogmatically and doing theological formulation along the same lines.
They provide a full description of their method and write that it "is
illumined by the Spirit, rooted in biblical exegesis, governed by patterns of biblical language, shaped by the biblical economy, guided by
the biblically derived rule of faith, guarded by biblically derived tradition, refined by systematic and philosophical reflection, and located
within the communion of the saints" (pp. 105, 141). They suggest that
each of these methodical considerations must be used to condition
theological judgments and that approaching theology in another way
may lead to less than biblical conclusions. Their trinitarian proposal
takes a fresh look at the Nicene-Constantinopolitan Creed to evaluate
its biblical faithfulness and modern applicability. Emerson and Stamps
specifically look at the language of *ousia* and *hypostases* along with
the three classical doctrinal pairings (One Nature / Three Persons,
One Will / Three Modes of Subsistence, and Inseparable Operations
/ Appropriation). Finally, they evaluate these doctrinal formulations
in light of the evangelical commitment to our Reformation heritage,
especially *sola scriptura*. They raise theological concerns with how
ERAS relates to the singularity of the divine will. In their response
chapter, they respond to Ware and Yarnell by clarifying their points of
commonality and distinction with both Yarnell and Ware. They open
their response by signifying that social trinitarian views of divine persons appear to inform Ware's appropriation of the analogy of being.
In addition to this initial concern, Emerson and Stamps respond to
Ware's chapter along canonical, confessional, and dogmatic lines to
raise distinct questions and further demonstrate the stability of their
method. They also question whether it is appropriate to distinguish, as
Yarnell does, between devotion-oriented monotheism and substance-
oriented monotheism. They express some misgivings that Yarnell does

not take a more decisive position on whether the Trinity is a model for complementarian relations between men and women.

The Importance of this Discussion

At the 2016 Southern Baptist Convention in St. Louis, Missouri, someone asked me if the current trinitarian debate over ERAS is really that important. I think the question that they were actually asking was, are these issues a matter of orthodoxy? Or, for Southern Baptists, does one's views in the debate impinge on the trinitarian doctrine set forth in the BF&M? This question is understandable, for some people have suggested that this discussion may touch the boundaries of our trinitarian faith. No one in this book denies the Christian teaching on the doctrine of the Trinity. The reflections in this book are in keeping with the historic teaching of the church and the BF&M.

Nevertheless, the contributors in this volume do hold opposing positions. They vary in how to conceive of the Trinity and how to theologize based on the doctrine of the Trinity. Their points of departure inflect their methodological commitments, which do not just relate to the *how* of theology but also to the *what* of theology. In this book, we have different ways of approaching the theological task and different visions for it, which have been on display throughout the larger debate over ERAS/EFS. For that reason, this interaction is important and has been profitable.

Theology is thinking about God and reflecting on how all things relate to him. Our God is triune. Thus, at the core of the theological task is disciplined, biblical thinking about the life of the triune God and how his triune nature impacts the nature and purpose of our lives. If that's true, and I think it is, then the most fundamental theological discussion is on how one formulates the Trinity. The reality is that evangelicals have not always embraced the Trinity's central role in theologizing. The Trinity has been treated as one doctrine of many. But, this doctrine is not just one article of faith among many other articles. It is the central article in which every other Christian doctrine is grounded and from which every other Christian doctrine is shaped and determined to be a "Christian confession." We have assumed the trinitarian formulation for generations, but we have not always thought deeply about what it means to proclaim that God is triune and how that informs everything else.

The purpose of this book is limited to interactions on trinitarian theology, one's theological method, and how both relate to one point of application. Yet the subject matter of this book casts a long shadow over our faith. The Trinity is central to the Christian faith, for the vibrancy of our churches, and for the clarity of our witness in the world. The heart of Christianity is trinitarian, because central to the salvation story is the relationship between the Father and the Son. This truth is captured simply by John in his Gospel, when he said, "God loved the world in this way: He gave his one and only Son, so that everyone who believes in him will not perish but have eternal life" (John 3:16 CSB). We may believe in the death of a man called Jesus. We may proclaim his bodily resurrection. We may trust his death and resurrection for our salvation. But without the doctrine of the Trinity, we are unable to believe that he is God and that his work is the very work of God. In addition, without the doctrine of the Trinity, we lose the significance of the Holy Spirit's work in the life of the believer. Because the Spirit is God, he too can make God known, and being divine, he unites believers to God when he indwells them. The bedrock of our faith is nothing less than God himself, and every aspect of the Christian story—creation, revelation, and salvation—is Christian only if it is understood to be the work of the triune God. This is reflected in the Apostles' and Athanasian creeds. These confessions are organized according to three articles, each extolling the nature and work of the triune God.

So the answer I gave to the question that I was asked in St. Louis, is "yes, it matters." Any time spent reflecting on the tri-unity of our

God and the ways he has revealed himself to us in the economy of salvation is important and worth the effort. If the differences among us
give us opportunity to reflect together on the centrality of the Trinity
in the Christian faith that is to our benefit. We sharpen each other
and serve the church in our rigorous and charitable interactions. This
book is about determining the best way to understand the relations of
the divine persons in the divine life and how that understanding rever-
berates throughout our theology. No doubt, much more can be said to
help us understand the nature of the triune God, the divine life, God's
working in the world, and how that informs all things.

I am thankful that some of my Southern Baptist colleagues agreed
that this was an important discussion. We have not always seen the
value of thinking together on what seems like finer points of theology.
Southern Baptists—a Bible-believing, gospel-centered, and mission-
focused people—should be eager to do this work, as we proclaim
the "triune God of the gospel" and the "gospel of the triune God."[17]
Bruce Ware helps by carefully demonstrating the fruit of his exegetical
labors in theological reflection, graciously listening to the critiques of
his view, and thoroughly answering the objection to his position with
reasoned theological responses. I am thankful that Malcolm Yarnell
frames this discussion (rightly) by prioritizing theology over anthropology, along with exemplifying a careful theological reading of Scripture
in his response chapter. Matthew Emerson and Luke Stamps serve us
by focusing our attention more directly on method. They propose that
the reading of Scripture unto trinitarian theologizing should be conditioned by pro-Nicene trinitarian grammar. I am honored that each
of the contributors would use their gifts to participate in this project.

---

[17] Kevin Vanhoozer and Daniel Treier, *Theology and the Mirror of Scripture*,
Studies in Christian Doctrine and Scripture (Downers Grove, IL: InterVarsity,
2015), 53–57.

I know each of them well. They all contributed to the project as an act of worship to the triune God because of their devotion to him.

Projects like this, however, do not happen without the supportive work of many people. Thank you also to Owen Kelly and Josh Alley for your help in preparing the manuscript. You both provided careful proofreading and insightful comments that have made this book better. Finally, to the team at B&H, Jim Baird, Chris Thompson, Audrey Greeson, and Sarah Landers, thank you for your support of the SBC Professor Fellowship, for editorial expertise, and for your patience as this project has taken a few unexpected turns. Ultimately, we give thanks to our triune God for revealing himself to us, and in the revelation of the Father and the Son, we receive eternal life (John 17:3).

Glory be to the Father, and to the Son:

and to the Holy Ghost;

As it was in the beginning, is now, and ever shall be:

world without end. Amen.[18]

---

[18] Ancient Christian prayer known as the *Glori Patri*.

CHAPTER 1

Unity and Distinction of the Trinitarian Persons

By Bruce A. Ware

Introduction: God as One and Three

The Christian faith affirms that God is one and that God is three: God is one in essence but three in persons. In essence, the Father, Son, and Holy Spirit are fully coequal and coeternal; in persons, the Father, Son, and Holy Spirit are different and distinct. These twin pillars, then, necessarily uphold the Christian doctrine of the Trinity: the *equality of the divine persons*, as each possesses fully and eternally the identically same one and undivided divine essence, and the *distinctiveness of the divine person*, as the Father, the Son, and the Spirit are distinguished hypostatically from each other. Both the oneness and the threeness of God are equally true and equally fundamental to who the one God truly is.

Christianity affirms this union of one and three. It rejects both unitarian monotheism (one but not three) and tritheism (three but not one), and it insists on trinitarian monotheism (three distinct

persons each of whom possesses eternally and fully the one and undivided divine nature). John 1:1 helps us see the crucial importance of
embracing these twin pillars of trinitarian doctrine. "In the beginning
was the Word, and the Word was with God [difference and distinc-
tion], and the Word was God [equality and identity]."[1]

The Oneness of God's Triune Being: Equality of Essence through an "Equality of Identity" among the Three Divine Persons

The oneness of God expresses the truth that there is one and only
one true and living God and one and only one eternal and undivided
divine essence, which possesses intrinsically every perfection or quality
in infinite measure. The oneness of God explains why Father, Son, and
Holy Spirit cannot rightly be conceived as three gods, for each possesses eternally and fully this one same and undivided divine essence.

The Father, the Son, and the Holy Spirit are equally God, for they
are identical in essence. The equality of the divine persons is the strongest kind of equality possible. Consider other kinds of equality in comparison to the unique equality that most importantly exists among the
three divine persons: (1) The equality that exists, for example, among
three evenly sliced pieces of pie is an *equality of proportionality*. Each piece
of pie is equal to the other pieces because each is the same proportion
of the total pie, that is, each is equally one-third of the pie. But the persons of the Trinity, though they possess an equality of proportionality—
each possesses 100 percent of the divine nature—have attached to
them an even stronger kind of equality. (2) Or the equality that exists
among creatures is, at best, an *equality of kind*—that is, two cats are
equal to each other, or two humans are equal to each other, because
each possesses the same kind of nature as the other. And although the

---

[1] Unless otherwise noted, all Scripture citations in this chapter are from the
New American Standard Bible (NASB).

persons of the Trinity are equal with an equality of kind—each indeed does possess a nature that is the same kind of nature as that which the other persons possess, since each possesses the same divine nature— their equality is not merely an equality of the same kind. (3) Rather, the unique equality that exists among the three persons of the Trinity is stronger yet than either an equality of proportionality or an equality of kind. It is an equality that appears to exist only among the distinct persons of the Godhead. Each divine person, in essence, possesses an *equality of identity* with the other divine persons precisely because all the divine persons possess identically the same nature. The Son is equal to the Father precisely because he possesses the identically same nature as the Father possesses—not merely a nature of the same proportion (100 percent of the divine nature) or the same kind (each possesses a divine nature), but the *very same and identical nature* as the Father possesses— as is affirmed by the Nicene Creed's declaration of the Son's being *homoousios* (same nature) with the Father. And the Spirit is equal to the Son and the Father precisely because he possesses the *very same and identical nature* as possessed by the Son and by the Father.

Because the Father, Son, and Spirit possess eternally the identi- cally same nature, each then must be understood as fully and in the strongest sense possible both coequal and coeternal—not three gods, but three personal expressions of the one and undivided divine nature that is commonly and fully possessed by each of the three divine per- sons. If the oneness of God is a oneness of the divine nature, where lies the distinctive threeness of God?

The Threeness of God's Triune Personhood: Distinction of Relations and Roles among the Fully Equal Divine Persons

The threeness of God expresses the truth that there are three distinct and distinguishable divine persons, each of whom possesses coequally and coeternally the identically one and undivided divine nature. For trinitarian doctrine, distinction of personhood is as necessary to maintain as unity or equality of nature or essence. While the Father possesses the identically same nature as the Son, the Father is not the Son and the Son is not the Father. While the Son possesses the identically same nature as the Spirit, the Son is not the Spirit and the Spirit is not the Son. And when one examines biblical indicators on the distinctiveness of the Father from the Son and Spirit, the Son from the Father and the Spirit, and the Spirit from the Father and the Son, one finds two categories that encompass the heart of their distinctiveness: *relation* and *role*.

Each is distinct most fundamentally in *ontological relation* due to the eternal relations of origin or modes of subsistence that identify each of the trinitarian persons uniquely. The Father (alone) is eternally unbegotten, the Son (alone) is eternally begotten by the Father, and the Spirit (alone) eternally proceeds from the Father and the Son (following Nicaea-Constantinople and the Western insertion of the *filioque*). These eternal relations of origin mark the fundamental distinction among the three persons,[2] and they also ground the functional relations that follow. Since the Father is eternally unbegotten while he also eternally begets the Son, the Father's unique hypostatic identity indeed is that of eternal Father; because the Son is eternally begotten by the Father, the Son's unique hypostatic identity indeed is that of eternal Son; and because the Spirit eternally proceeds from the Father and the Son, the Spirit's unique hypostatic identity indeed is that of the eternal Spirit. These three distinct hypostatic identities, then, are not interchangeable, nor are they true merely of the economic Trinity

---

[2] These eternal relations of origin also relate to the unity and equality of the three persons insofar as the Nicene fathers understood the One who is begotten to possess the same nature as the One who begets, and the One who proceeds to possess the same nature as the One(s) from whom he proceeds. Hence, the Son's being *homoousios* with the Father is tied closely to, and is expressive of, the Son being eternally begotten of the Father.

ad extra; rather, they are the eternal, unchangeable, fixed hypostatic identities of the persons of the immanent Trinity *ad intra*. This leads to the second way Scripture identifies distinctions among the trinitarian persons.

The trinitarian persons are also distinct in *functional relation* within the Godhead such that each expresses outwardly, as it were, who he is ontologically and hypostatically as defined by and flowing from their respective eternal relations of origin. Since the Father's unique hypostatic identity is that of the eternally unbegotten Father, he then eternally acts in a manner that befits who he is as Father; because the Son's unique hypostatic identity is that of the eternally begotten Son of the Father, the Son always acts in a manner that befits who he is as Son; and because the Spirit's unique hypostatic identity is as the One who eternally proceeds from the Father and the Son, the Spirit eternally acts in a manner that befits One who comes from and is united with both the Father and the Son. This may seem an obvious point to make, but it should be made explicit nonetheless. Because the Father is *Father* by his mode of subsistence as eternally unbegotten and begetter of the Son, he never acts as the Son or as the Spirit; he always, eternally, in all expressions of his personhood, acts as what he is, Father. The same must be said of the Son and the Spirit also: they always, eternally, in all expressions of their personhood, act as what they are, Son and Spirit respectively. So, though their action is unified as carried out always through the one and undivided divine nature,[3] their action is also distinct, since each of them acts according to their respective hypostatic identities and never apart from them.

Biblically this relational and functional distinction of persons is most evident in the Father-Son relation in part because of what is conveyed by their respective divine names. The names of "Father" and

---

[3] I will discuss below the doctrine of the inseparability of the divine actions *ad extra* with further argumentation for why action of the trinitarian persons must rightly be seen as inseparable yet not as indistinguishable.

"Son" are not ad hoc, nor are they true merely of the economic Trinity since they are attached to the eternal relations of origin whereby the Father is the eternally unbegotten Father of the Son, and the Son is the eternally begotten Son of the Father. Hence, "Father" names the One who is the eternal Father of the Son, and "Son" names the One who is the eternal Son of the Father. That is, they are distinct, and their distinction is manifest in part by their hypostatically distinct, eternal, and noninterchangeable divine names along with what those divine names signal. Note that these persons of the Trinity, then, are not brother, brother, brother or friend, friend, friend. Rather, as the three-person triune God is eternally named, they are none other than Father, Son, and Spirit.[4]

The very identity, then, of the first person of the Trinity is seen in and through his relation as the Father of the Son, and hence he functions always in a paternal way toward his Son. Likewise, the very identity of the second person of the Trinity is seen precisely through and not apart from his being the Son of the Father, and hence he functions always in a filial way toward his Father. The Spirit, since he proceeds from the Father and the Son, functionally relates as agent of the Father and the Son. In other words, while the Father, Son, and Spirit are unitedly the One God, acting from the commonly possessed divine nature, they also eternally act from their distinctive hypostatic identities: the Father acts only and always as *God . . . the Father*; the Son acts only and always as *God . . . the Son*; the Spirit acts only and always as *God . . . the Spirit*. Because their ontological relations are eternal and unchangeable, so are their functional relations likewise eternal and unchangeable.

Scripture further demonstrates, as I will defend more fully below, the Father's distinctive functional relation to the Son, in part, contains

---

[4] To deny this claim is to entertain some notion of "god" behind the God of revelation, which inevitably leads to agnosticism. If the word of God truly is the self-revelation of God, then God is none other than Father, Son, and Holy Spirit, and he is so eternally.

the expression of paternal authority in this relationship, and the Son's distinctive functional relation to the Father, in part, contains the expression of filial submission. Eternal paternal authority and eternal filial submission give expression, therefore, to a portion of the meaning contained within the divine personal names of Father and Son, which in turn flow from their eternal hypostatic identities as eternal Father and eternal Son, which in turn flow from their respective eternal relations of origin. The Spirit likewise evidences a submissive functional relation to both the Father and the Son, expressing his mode of subsistence as proceeding from the Father and the Son. So then, relation—both ontological and functional expressions of relation—is a central category for understanding the distinctions between the three persons of the Trinity.

These distinct relations give expression to unique *roles* that each divine person carries out economically. Although all three work together in harmonious unity, as the early church fathers' doctrine of the inseparable operations (*opera ad extra omnia sunt indivisa*) affirms, each divine person contributes distinctively to this unified work of one God. John Calvin warns us that we dare not miss this hypostatic distinction in the divine work.

> It is not fitting to suppress the distinction that we observe to be expressed in Scripture. It is this: to the Father is attributed the beginning of activity, and the fountain and wellspring of all things; to the Son, wisdom, counsel, and the ordered disposition of all things; but to the Spirit is assigned the power and efficacy of that activity. . . . [T]he observance of an order is not meaningless or superfluous, when the Father is thought of first, then from him the Son, and finally from both the Spirit.[5]

---

[5] John Calvin, *Institutes of the Christian Religion* 1:13.18, ed. John T. McNeill, trans. Ford Lewis Battles, Library of Christian Classics, vol. 20 (Philadelphia: Westminster, 1960), 142–43.

The Father carries out different and differing roles and activities than do
the Son and the Spirit, and the same can be said for each of the other persons as well. To give some obvious examples, only the Father (not the Son
or the Spirit) sends the Son into the world; only the Son (not the Father
or the Spirit) becomes incarnate; and only the Spirit (not the Father or
the Son) comes at Pentecost as sent from the Father and the Son.

Those in the pro-Nicene tradition commonly refer here to the
doctrine of appropriations in which the order of operations among
the divine persons depends on the order of their subsistence in the triune Being.[6] For example, that the Father sends the Son expresses the
appropriation of sending to the Father by virtue of the Son's mode of
subsistence as the begotten of the Father. The sending of the Spirit by
the Father and the Son is the expression of the appropriation of sending to the Father and Son by virtue of the Spirit's mode of subsistence
as proceeding from the Father and the Son. That is, the external works
of the trinitarian persons are always expressive of their eternal modes
of subsistence or eternal relations of origin.

I fully agree with the pro-Nicene doctrine of appropriations and
find it biblical and right to depict the divine trinitarian operations
as expressive of their eternal modes of subsistence. Yet, while what I
affirm in this chapter fully accords with this pro-Nicene understanding, I believe that the appeal to divine appropriations falls short of
expressing fully what Scripture indicates regarding the functional relations and operations of the trinitarian persons. Yes, the order of operations *ad extra* is expressive of the order of relations *ad intra*, but saying
only this excludes a significant portion of scriptural indications. When
one considers the Father sending the Son, though it is true that the
Father acts as sender due to his manner of subsisting, to leave it here
misses also the personal planning, motives, purposes, and authority

---

[6] For an incisive discussion and analysis of the doctrine of appropriations,
see Adonis Vidu, "Trinitarian Inseparable Operations and the Trinity," *Journal of
Analytic Theology* 4 (2016): 106–27.

the Father exhibits in his sending of the Son. The act of the Father sending the Son is not some kind of mechanical or impersonal out-working of the relations of origin; rather, it is an intensely personal action—the action of a genuine Father who is about to send his only begotten and deeply beloved Son to endure excruciating pain and death, and he does this out of his great love for those sinners whose rescue can take place only through what his Son, and no one else, can do. The pathos, the reality, the plans and purposes, the motives, and, yes, the authority and submission of the Father's sending and the Son's glad and willing descent to a sinful earth are deeply imbedded in the biblical story in a way that mere appeal to the doctrine of appropria-tions misses. We must hear the Scriptures and notice the distinctive trinitarian operations in which these expressions of motive, purpose, authority, submission, joy, and longing attach to the very persons of the Godhead in the outworking of the unified work of the one God.

In summary then, what distinguishes the three persons from each other within the Godhead? Their distinctive relations—both ontologi-cal and functional—and roles are the clearest expressions of just how each is distinct from the others and the features that constitute the uniqueness of each divine person. The doctrine of the Trinity, then, is an accounting and expression of both (1) the one, undivided divine nature eternally and fully possessed by each of the three divine persons, and (2) each member's distinct personhood, according to the eternal relations of origin, such that each has his own unique relation with the other members, and each carries out distinctive roles in a manner that accords with the hypostatic distinctiveness of the Father, the Son, and the Holy Spirit.

Biblical Support for Trinitarian Distinctiveness Expressive of Relations and Roles

My focus for the remainder of this chapter is to describe and defend this thesis: while the categories of "relations" and "roles" are the clearest and most comprehensive in undergirding that which distinguishes the Father from the Son and from the Spirit, within these relations,[7] and expressed in their respective roles, one finds a prevailing authority-submission structure that gives order and direction to the roles carried out by the three trinitarian persons.

To be more precise, one finds the Father, who in ontological relation is eternally Father of the Son, acting, then, in a manner befitting his paternal hypostatic identity by planning, designing, commanding, sending, purposing, willing, and so forth, all that takes place through the Son and the Spirit. One finds the Son, who in ontological relation is eternally begotten of the Father, acting in a manner befitting his filial hypostatic identity to the Father by obeying, going, doing, accomplishing, working, and so forth, all that the Father has given him to do. And one finds the Spirit, who functions as the agent of the Son, in fulfilling the work assigned by the Father, always acting in a manner that befits his role by assisting, empowering, enlivening, enacting, and so forth, all that the Father and Son have directed him to do. While the theologians of the early church often spoke of the *taxis* (order) among the trinitarian persons, referring centrally to their eternal relations of origin, what they did not as often describe is the functional relations of authority and submission expressive of and grounded on these widely accepted eternal relations of origin. Some saw this, however. For example, Hilary of Poitiers, writing in the mid-fourth century, affirms that

> [I]n spite of the fact that both the Unborn Father is God and the Only-begotten Son of God is God, God is nevertheless One, and the subjection and dignity of the Son are both taught in that by being called Son He is made subject to that name which because it implies that God is His Father is yet a name which denotes His

---

[7] I have in mind largely the functional relations among the trinitarian persons, which are grounded on the eternal relations of origin or modes of subsistence, as indicated above, and will be discussed more at the end of this chapter.

nature. Having a name which belongs to Him whose Son He is,
He is subject to the Father both in service and name; yet in such
a way that the subordination of His name bears witness to the
true character of His natural and exactly similar essence.[8]

What Hilary spoke of here one also finds throughout the biblical
record of the self-revelation of trinitarian relations and roles, namely,
that this ontological trinitarian *taxis* is expressive also of a functional
structure of authority and submission among the trinitarian persons.

To facilitate my discussion and defense of this thesis, I will make
an appeal to the opening two verses of the book of Hebrews (with
several other texts also considered) as a guide to observing biblically
normative and uniform trinitarian relations and roles. I will discuss the
Father's relation to the Son as it is manifest in the work of the Son in
eternity past, in the incarnation, and through eternity future, and we
will also observe what these opening verses indicate about the role of
the Spirit vis-à-vis the Father and the Son. Please note that, as I appeal
to this and several other passages in what follows, I will discuss these
texts using language that reflects what these passages say. For example,
I'll talk about one or another trinitarian person speaking or creating
or willing or initiating or doing or implementing or obeying, because
such language reflects the way the authors of Scripture have chosen to
speak. I am aware that in some cases, this way of speaking may sound
different than, even contrary to, how some in the pro-Nicene tradition
prefer to speak of the triune persons given commitments to inseparable divine operations *ad extra* and one will in God. But since the Bible is
our sole ultimate and only absolute authority for knowing rightly who
God is, we must listen carefully to how it speaks and only then seek
to understand how this way of speaking may fit with how many of the

---

[8] Hilary of Poitiers (ca. 300–368), *On the Councils* 51, in A Select Library of
Nicene and Post-Nicene Fathers of the Christian Church: 2nd series, vol. 9, ed.
Philip Schaff (Grand Rapids, MI: Eerdmans, 1952–57), 18–19.

early church fathers understood the divine will and action. Following our biblical survey based on Heb 1:1–2, I will close the chapter with responses to several issues that have been raised to this proposed linkage of eternal functional trinitarian relations of authority and submission as expressive of the eternal trinitarian relations of origin.

Our examination of biblical teaching on the trinitarian persons' relations and roles begins with the opening verses (vv. 1–2) of the book of Hebrews:

> God, after He spoke long ago to the fathers in the prophets in many portions and in many ways, in these last days has spoken to us in His Son, whom He appointed heir of all things, through whom also He made the world.

These brief verses provide something of a template for understanding the relations and roles among the trinitarian persons. Intrinsic to these relations and roles is the central place that the authority and submission structure has in understanding just how and why the Father, Son, and Spirit function in the ways they do. Observe with me five features that we can derive from these opening verses.

The Father Is the Subject of the Verbs in Heb 1:1–2. First, the primacy of the Father is highlighted in how these opening verses are written. Note the subject and verb in each of the clauses:[9]

> God . . . spoke long ago to the fathers (1a)
> God . . . has spoken to us in His Son (2a)
> God . . . appointed [the Son] heir of all things (2b)
> God . . . made the world [through the Son] (2c)

---

[9] Paul Ellingworth, *The Epistle to the Hebrews: A Commentary on the Greek Text*, New International Greek Testament Commentary (Grand Rapids, MI: Eerdmans, 1993), 89, writes of Heb 1:1–2, "Grammatically, this carefully composed opening sentence consists of a participial phrase (v. 1), the main clause (v. 2a), and two subordinate clauses (v. 2b), all with God as their subject. . . . The verbs in vv. 1–2 have God as their subject."

And if there is any doubt that "God" here is the Father, this question is answered when we read that "God" has spoken "in His Son." Since the one God, the triune God, does not have a Son, and since the Son does not have a Son, and since the Spirit does not have a Son, this must be a reference to God the Father who has spoken in his Son. So, without any question, the design of these opening verses is to stress the primary place of the Father who performed each of these actions through others.

The chapter as a whole is written to present the supremacy of Jesus.[10] The next two verses (vv. 3–4) switch focus to the Son as the subject and central figure. But verses 1–2 establish that all the Son does, in his work in eternity past, in the incarnation, and in eternity future, is owing to the direction, plan, purpose, and activity of the Father who speaks his word and does his work through the Son. Hebrews stresses the word and work of the Father, through the agency of the Son (and the Spirit, as we'll see below) at the outset.

The Father Speaks through the Incarnate Son. The second feature to observe from Heb 1:1–2 is that the incarnate Son's teaching consists, behind his own words, of the words of the Father. When we read that the Father "has spoken to us in His Son" (1:2a), one might think that this has to do more with the fact that the Son reveals the Father in the character of his life and in the way that he lives. Many other passages bear this out. Even Heb 1:3, with its emphasis on the very character and activity of the Son manifesting the very nature and glory of the Father, would support this view. Add to this John 1:14, 18; 10:30; and 14:9, and you have strong reason to conclude that the character and ministry of the Son reflected beautifully and exactly the very character and nature of the Father.

But I suspect more is being conveyed by saying the Father "has spoken to us in His Son." In light of the prior reference to the Father

---

[10] See Peter T. O'Brien, *The Letter to the Hebrews*, Pillar New Testament Commentary, ed. D. A. Carson (Grand Rapids, MI: Eerdmans, 2010), 46.

speaking long ago to the fathers in the prophets (1:1), it would seem
that the statement in verse 2 includes not only the general ways in
which the Son displayed the character and nature of the Father, but
also that the Son came and spoke accurately and truthfully the very
word that the Father gave him to speak. That is, the teaching of the
Son originated in the Father, not in himself, although the Son fully
embodied that teaching and spoke it with full conviction and authority. Indeed, the Father's word was his word (e.g., John 16:15), yet the
primacy is given here to the Father whose word is spoken through his
Son. Adding to this, if we recall Jesus's claim that he was not speaking
his own word but the word of the Father who sent him (e.g., John 8:28;
14:10), we realize that Jesus understood his purpose was not to originate the message he came to deliver, but rather to depend fully on the
Father to provide him with what he was to speak.

John 14:9–10 puts these two ideas together beautifully, where Jesus
says to Philip, "He who has seen Me has seen the Father" (v. 9) but
then follows with "The words that I say to you I do not speak on My
own initiative, but the Father abiding in Me does His works" (v. 10). So
the very character of Christ displays the character of the Father (v. 9),
but also the very words of Christ display the very words of the Father
(v. 10). The Father originates these words, according to Jesus. Jesus
speaks what the Father gives him to speak.

This is in keeping with the more general teaching of the Gospels
that the Son came for the purpose of doing and fulfilling the work of
the Father. One of the most beautiful expressions of this is found in
John 4:34, where Jesus has just declined food offered to him, saying,
"My food is to do the will of Him who sent Me and to accomplish His
work." Everything the Son did, said, and accomplished was in direct
obedience to the will of the Father, right down to his choice to go to
the cross, praying, "Father, if You are willing, remove this cup from Me;
yet not My will, but Yours be done" (Luke 22:42).

The summary statement in Heb 1:2, that the Father has spoken
to us in his Son, should be understood to refer to the character of the

Father reflected in the Son, the words of the Father spoken by the Son, and the very purpose and will of the Father accomplished by the Son. The incarnate life of this Son was marked by an obedience to the will of his Father that was unbroken for the entirety of his life and ministry, as summarized by Jesus with the words, "I always do the things that are pleasing to Him" (John 8:29).

The Father Appoints the Son over All Things for All of Eternity Future. The third feature to observe from Heb 1:1–2 is that the authority of the Father over the Son is not limited to the incarnation, but rather extends into eternity future with the everlasting reign of the Son over the world and the new creation, as Hebrews declares that the Father "appointed [the Son] heir of all things" (v. 2).[11] Hebrews 1:2 might have made the point more generally that Jesus would be heir of all things or that he would reign as the one in highest position over all things, without specifying the role of the Father in placing him in this position. But clearly Hebrews intends more than this. The author intends also to convey that the Son has this authority and reigns as heir over all as the result of the Father granting him this very place above all. Again, we see the authority of the Father exercised as the Father grants his Son the position of exclusive universal heir.

This explicit reference to the authority of the Father over the Son, in appointing him heir of all things, makes a stronger statement than any reference to the authority of the Father over the Son in the incarnation. The Father's authority is surely rightly derived from the claim that the Father "in these last days has spoken to us in His Son" (1:2a). However, the assertion of the Father's authority over Christ, regarding what is given to him in his resurrection, ascension, and coronation as he sits at the right hand of the Father (1:3b) to reign, is more explicit and direct because the Father has "appointed [him] heir of all things" (1:2b).

---

[11] George H. Guthrie, *Hebrews: The NIV Application Commentary* (Grand Rapids, MI: Zondervan, 1998), 47, suggests that this is likely a reference to Ps 2:7.

Many passages confirm the Father's appointment of the Son. Consider, from this sampling of passages (emphasis added), the breadth of the biblical teaching that the messianic Son now exercises and enjoys the position of rulership and authority over all of creation because the Father has given them to his risen and exalted Son:

> Psalm 2:7–9 – "I will surely tell of the decree of the LORD: / He said to Me, 'You are My Son, / Today I have begotten You. / 'Ask of Me, and *I will surely give the nations as Your inheritance, / And the very ends of the earth as Your possession.* / 'You shall break them with a rod of iron, / You shall shatter them like earthenware.'" (quoted in Acts 13:33 of the risen Christ)

> Psalm 110:1 – The LORD says to my Lord: / "Sit at My right hand / Until *I make Your enemies a footstool for Your feet.*" (quoted in Acts 2:33–36 of the risen Christ)

> Matthew 28:18–20 – And Jesus came up and spoke to them, saying, *"All authority has been given to Me in heaven and on earth.* Go therefore and make disciples of all the nations, baptizing them in the name of the Father and the Son and the Holy Spirit, teaching them to observe all that I commanded you; and lo, I am with you always, even to the end of the age."[12]

> 1 Corinthians 15:25–28 – For He must reign until He has put all His enemies under His feet. The last enemy that will be abolished is death. For HE HAS PUT ALL THINGS IN SUBJECTION UNDER HIS FEET. *But when He says, "All things are put in subjection," it is evident that He [the Father] is excepted who put all things in subjection to Him [the Son].* When all things are subjected to

---

[12] On the authority implied in the order of the divine personal names, see Simon J. Gathercole, *The Pre-Existent Son: Recovering the Christologies of Matthew, Mark, and Luke* (Grand Rapids, MI: Eerdmans, 2006), 72–73.

Him, then the *Son Himself also will be subjected to the One who subjected all things to Him,* so that God may be all in all.

Ephesians 1:20–23 – He [the Father] raised Him [the Son] from the dead and *seated Him at His right hand* in the heavenly places, far above all rule and authority and power and dominion, and every name that is named, not only in this age but also in the one to come. And *He [the Father] put all things in subjection under His [the Son's] feet and gave Him [the Son] as head over all things to the church,* which is His body, the fullness of Him who fills all in all.

Philippians 2:8–11 – Being found in appearance as a man, He humbled Himself by becoming obedient to the point of death, even death on a cross. *For this reason also, God highly exalted Him, and bestowed on Him the name which is above every name,* so that at the name of Jesus EVERY KNEE WILL BOW, of those who are in heaven and on earth and under the earth, and that every tongue will confess that Jesus Christ is Lord, to the glory of God the Father.

Hebrews 2:8–9 – "YOU HAVE PUT ALL THINGS IN SUBJECTION UNDER HIS FEET." For *in subjecting all things to him, He left nothing that is not subject to him.* But now we do not yet see all things subjected to him. But we do see Him who was made for a little while lower than the angels, namely, Jesus, because of the suffering of death crowned with glory and honor, so that by the grace of God He might taste death for everyone.

1 Peter 3:21–22 – Corresponding to that, baptism now saves you—not the removal of dirt from the flesh, but an appeal to God for a good conscience—through the resurrection of Jesus Christ, who is at the right hand of God, having gone into heaven, *after angels and authorities and powers had been subjected to Him.*

These texts provide additional support to the brief but very powerful statement in Heb 1:2, that the Father has "appointed [His Son] heir of all things." The authority that the Father exercised in the incarnate Son's teaching and ministry now shows forcefully as the Father grants the messianic Son vice-regency, seating the Son at his right hand, over all of creation.

The Father Creates through His Eternal Son. The fourth feature to observe from Heb 1:1–2 expresses the creation of the world *by* the Father *through* his Son. It would have been easy for the writer of Hebrews to declare, simply and straightforwardly, that the Son (with no mention of the Father) is the creator of all things. Imagine him writing, "in these last days the Father has spoken to us in his Son, whom he appointed heir of all things, who also made the world." Instead, the final phrase of verse 2 is "through whom also He made the world." Given the clarity of John 1:3 and Col 1:16, it would be a natural and accurate summary comment to assert the Son as creator. But Hebrews continues its pattern: the author indicates the primacy of the Father in the work of the Son by adding that the Son acted as the agent of the Father in eternity past when the Father fashioned the world through his Son.

Does the phrase "through whom also He made the world" signal authority and submission? I would argue yes. The authority of the Father and the submission of the Son are conceptually contained within this final phrase of verse 2. Consider these factors:

(1) This final phrase comes at the end of the opening two verses of Hebrews that have emphasized the priority of the Father. The Father has spoken through prophets of old, the Father has spoken in and through his incarnate Son, the Father has appointed the Son heir of all, and now Hebrews declares that the Father created the world through the Son. Each of the preceding three statements involves the Father in a relation of authority, first over the prophets who speak the Father's word, then over the Son who likewise speaks as divine spokesman of the Father, and third over the Son as he appoints him heir

over all things. This pattern would argue for continuing the same kind of relation that has been stressed, a relation marked by the ultimate authority of the Father in what takes place in creation. How appropriate for the Father now to be seen in this role, having authority over the very beginning of creation, as the initiator, planner, designer, and architect of creation, who then assigns the building or crafting of this creation to his own Son.[13]

(2) If authority and submission are absent, what is the point of saying that the Father creates through the Son? If the work of the two persons is purely collaborative, or strictly unitive, it would be misleading to state that creation happened by one person through another person. For creation to be by one person yet through another person requires that the former have the place of primacy in just what creation should be, while the other person acts on and implements what is given him to do. It seems disingenuous to say that the Father made the world through the Son if the Father and Son together were responsible in the identically same ways for just what that creation would be. To the contrary, the author of Hebrews maintains the pattern of the primacy of the Father; the most natural and only fully satisfying explanation is the ultimate authority of the Father, whose design and plan is implemented by the Son.

(3) This view finds resonance with other New Testament teaching of how creation occurred. For example, 1 Cor 8:6 says, "yet for us there is but one God, the Father, from whom are all things and we exist for Him; and one Lord, Jesus Christ, by whom are all things, and we exist through Him." The prepositions are crucial: creation comes *from* the Father and *through* the Son. What we do not have here is "from the Father and the Son" and "through the Father and the Son." The priority is with the Father, from whom creation comes as he plans and purposes just what creation will be; the Son functions here, as he

---

[13] Cf. Thomas R. Schreiner, *Commentary on Hebrews*, Biblical Theology for Proclamation (Nashville, TN: B&H, 2015), 55.

does everywhere, as the agent carrying out the will and executing the plan of the Father. Or consider John 1:1–3, in which we hear echoes of Genesis 1 where God creates by his speech. Whereas in Genesis 1 God creates by speaking, in John 1 God creates by his Word. As John writes, "All things were created through him . . ." (John 1:3 CSB). The Father creates the world through the Son, who is the Father's agent of creation.

This pattern fits other aspects of the Father-Son relation in eternity past. The sending language in John's Gospel provides one of the strongest evidences of the Father's eternal authority over his eternal Son.[14] Roughly forty times we are told the Father sent the Son into the world; to the Father is assigned the plan and purpose of the Son's coming, and to the Son is assigned his full willingness to follow what the Father has called him and sent him to do. Several passages from John address the sending of the Son by the Father.

> John 3:16–17 – For God so loved the world, that He gave His only begotten Son, that whoever believes in Him shall not perish, but have eternal life. For God did not send the Son into the world to judge the world, but that the world might be saved through Him.

We must begin by reminding ourselves that only God the Father has a Son—an only begotten Son—so "God" in John 3:16–17 must be God the Father. What do these verses indicate, if anything, about the primacy of God the Father among the trinitarian persons? (1) The Father has ontological primacy as the Father who eternally begets his Son. The Johannine "begotten" language here has been disputed, but it seems like it very well may be that this is the best rendering of John's

---

[14] See the very helpful discussion by Christopher W. Cowan, "'I Always Do What Pleases Him': The Father and Son in the Gospel of John," in *One God in Three Persons: Unity of Essence, Distinction of Persons, Implications for Life*, ed. Bruce A. Ware and John Starke (Wheaton, IL: Crossway, 2015), 47–64.

intention with *monogenes*.[15] The reference to giving his only begotten Son indicates that he has paternal priority in relation to the Son as the One who has begotten this Son. (2) One sees the motive of the Father here, which must be exclusively the Father's even if his motive is in concert with or united with the motives of the Son and Spirit. Here the Father is said to love the world to such a degree that he gave his only begotten Son. This love is of necessity distinct from the love the Son has in coming, and from the love the Spirit has in empowering the Son's mission. Only the Father could be moved by his great love to give his own Son, because only the Father has a Son to give (see 1 John 4:10 for a parallel statement). (3) The Father's distinct purpose is also evident from verse 17, which could be paraphrased to read, "God did not send the Son into the world for the purpose of judging the world, but rather for this purpose: that the world might be saved through him." Again, since only the Father has a Son to send, only the Father could have this precise purpose, even if his purpose was fully consonant with the Son's purpose in coming. (4) Paternal authority is necessary here to account for the significance of the Father giving and sending his only begotten Son. Denying paternal authority in the giving and sending of the Son diminishes, if not demolishes, the weightiness and significance of the Father's distinct motive and the Father's distinct purpose, both of which are tied specifically to the Father's offering the gift of his only begotten Son.

> John 6:38 – For I have come down from heaven, not to do My own will, but the will of Him who sent Me.

---

[15] A recent paper by Lee Irons provides compelling support for the traditional understanding of *monogenes* as meaning "only begotten." "A Lexical Defense of the Eternal Generation of the 'Only-Begotten' Son" was first delivered as a paper at the Far West Regional meeting of the Evangelical Theological Society, April 11, 2014, and published in the anthology *Retrieving Eternal Generation*, ed. Fred Sanders and Scott R. Swain (Grand Rapids, MI: Zondervan, 2017).

This is a remarkable statement from Jesus and a clear declaration that he is doing the Father's will (specifically) in his mission on earth. Notice a couple of features: (1) Saying "I have come down from heaven" indicates the plan and will of the Father in eternity past, prior to the incarnation, which the Son carries out in his coming from heaven to earth. This is not merely a statement of the Son's submission to the Father once he has become incarnate and begins ministering on earth; rather, this indicates the eternal Son's submission to the will of the Father in coming down from heaven to become incarnate in the first place. (2) In saying, "not to do My own will," the Son, in some sense, distinguishes the Father's will from his own; furthermore, he declares that he does not carry out his own will but the will of the Father. Jesus did not have to include the middle clause of this verse. He could have simply declared, "For I have come down from heaven to do the will of Him who sent Me." This is true and would also indicate the submission of the Son to the will of the Father. By including the middle clause, Jesus goes out of his way to distinguish his and his Father's wills, asserting his purpose to accomplish the latter. This does not require that we see these two "wills" in conflict or even as disunited. The Son fully and joyously embraces the will of his Father (see also John 4:34), but his point is one of initiation or origination. The Father, not the Son, is the divine agent who plans and designs the purpose of the incarnate life, ministry, death, resurrection, exaltation, and reign of the Son. Jesus is simply making clear that the will he embraces is not initiated by him but by his Father. The Father is the grand architect and wise designer of all that takes place in creation, redemption, and the new creation. Hence the Son does not devise his own purpose in coming, but gladly accepts what the Father has designed for him.[16]

---

[16] See below for a discussion of how there can be a will of the Father distinct from the will of the Son in the Godhead where all three persons share fully together the one and undivided divine nature with one divine will.

John 8:42 – I proceeded forth and have come from God, for
I have not even come on My own initiative, but He sent Me.

We see here a parallel statement to John 6:38, and the two points
just discussed should be affirmed here as well. (1) To say "I proceeded
forth and have come from God" indicates his coming to earth, sent by
the Father, to become incarnate. It cannot be reduced merely to the
Son's submission once he is already on earth. His submission on earth
continues the submission of the Son in coming "from God" or being
"sent" by God. (2) Once again, the middle clause is not necessary to
make the basic point. Jesus could have said, "I proceeded forth and
have come from God who sent Me." This would have been entirely
true and valid for him to have said. But he does not settle for this more
minimalist statement but asserts also, "for I have not even come on
My own initiative." Again, there is no conflict here between what the
Father sends the Son to do and what the Son actively and gladly does.
The Son fully embraces the plan and purpose of the Father in sending
him. But his point is one of initiation; I did not initiate my own coming, declares Jesus, I have come from the one who initiated, from the
one who sent me.

John 10:36 – do you say of Him, whom the Father sanctified
and sent into the world, "You are blaspheming," because I said,
"I am the Son of God"?

Here we have another declaration from Jesus indicating that in
eternity past, prior to the incarnation of the Son, the Father "sanctified and sent" his Son into the world. Jesus is asserting his own deity,
claiming that he does not blaspheme when he declares, "I am the Son
of God." But he uses for his defense the notion that he is sent by the
Father, who "sanctified" him to come. The term "sanctified" here must
refer not to some supposed purification of Jesus (he was without sin
before, during, and after his earthly incarnate life), but to his being
"set apart" for the work the Father sent him to do. Once again, Jesus

does not speak merely of coming to earth, but of coming as the Father *set him apart* and *sent him* into the world. That he has come from the Father shows he is one with the Father, and hence the charge of blasphemy is rejected.

Not only John's Gospel but also the Synoptics speak of the Father sending the Son, and the Father and Son sending the Spirit, in a manner depicting the authority of the sender and submission of the one sent. Commenting particularly on the significance of the order of the divine names in Matt 28:19, Simon Gathercole writes,

> We have already seen how in Mark 13.32 Jesus stands between God and the angels in a heavenly hierarchy; in Matt. 28.19, however, we have a *divine* hierarchy of Father, Son, and Spirit: all three persons participate in the divine name invoked in baptism.
>
> Already within the context of earliest Christianity, there is significance in the *order* of the names, however. Very common in the Synoptics is the implication of the Father's authority over the Son and the corresponding obedience of the Son to the Father. All things are given to the Son by his Father (Matt. 11.27 par. Luke 10.22; Matt. 28.18), and he continues to depend on the Father in prayer (e.g. Mark 1.35). Perhaps most clearly of all, the Son is frequently described as *sent* by the Father: once or twice in Mark, twice in Matthew, four times in Luke. Sending clearly presupposes an authority of the sender over the envoy.
>
> In terms of the Son's authority over the Spirit, in John and Acts it is evident that the Son sends the Spirit (John 15.26; cf. 14.26; Acts 2.33). Jesus' sending of the Spirit at Pentecost would have been understood as the fulfillment of John the Baptist's promise (common to all four Gospels) that Jesus would baptize with the Holy Spirit. This itself presupposes divine identity: as Jenson rightly notes, "No prophet as such can do this.

To give the Spirit is to act from the position of God." But if the Son is the one who *sends* the Spirit, then this again would pre- suppose a relationship of hierarchy within a Jewish context. As a result, it can be concluded that the order Father-Son-Spirit in Matt. 28.19 is not incidental; rather, it is born out of the early Christian thinking that the Father has authority over the Son, who in turn has authority over the Spirit.[17]

God the Son, then, is both God and Son. As *God*, he is fully equal with God the Father, in that both Father and Son possess fully the identically same and eternal divine nature. Therefore, the equality between the Father and Son (and Spirit) could not be stronger—as we saw above, they possess an equality of identity (i.e., each possesses fully the identically same divine nature). As *Son*, the Son is eternally the Son of the Father. As Son of the Father, he is under the authority of his Father and seeks in all he does to act as the agent of the Father's will, working and doing all that the Father has purposed and designed for his Son to accomplish. The eternal Son, God the Son, is both *fully God* and fully equal to the Father and at the same time he is *fully Son* and eternally in a relation of agency to the Father, carrying out the work and implementing the will of the Father in full submission and obedi- ence to all that the Father has planned. God and Son (i.e., fully God in nature and fully Son in person)—this is the Second Person of the Trinity that Hebrews, John, and the New Testament declare.

The Father Spoke in the Past through the Holy Spirit. The fifth and last feature to observe from Heb 1:1–2 is that the primacy and authority of the Father is also implied in Heb 1:1 in relation to the Spirit. The opening claim of verse 1, "[God] spoke long ago to the fathers in the

---

[17] Simon J. Gathercole, *The Pre-Existent Son: Recovering the Christologies of Matthew, Mark, and Luke* (Grand Rapids, MI: Eerdmans, 2006), 72–73. Gathercole's quo- tation of Jenson is from R. W. Jenson, *Systematic Theology*, vol. 1, *The Triune God* (Oxford: Oxford University Press, 1997), 88.

prophets in many portions and in many ways," is somewhat startling in light of the many passages that indicate that the Spirit is the one who moves and directs the prophets of old to speak the word of the Lord. The classic text is 2 Pet 1:21, which asserts, "for no prophecy of Scripture was ever made by an act of human will, but men moved by the Holy Spirit spoke from God." We also see the Spirit moving the prophets of God to speak the word of God elsewhere. The author of Hebrews, well aware of this, writes, "Therefore, just as the Holy Spirit says," before quoting Ps 95:7–11 (Heb 3:7). Likewise, later in the book, Hebrews declares, "And the Holy Spirit also testifies to us" (Heb 10:15), followed by a quotation from Jer 31:33–34.

So who speaks through the prophets, the Father or the Spirit? It seems likely that, to answer this question, we must appeal to a relation the Father has with the Spirit that is similar in kind to the relation the Father has with his Son.[18] That is, just as the Son is agent of the Father, so also is the Spirit agent of the Father. This seems to be implied in 2 Pet 1:21, quoted above—"men moved by the Holy Spirit spoke *from God*" (emphasis added). Since the Holy Spirit is the agent of the Father in his role of empowering, enlightening, and revealing, the Spirit's moving of biblical prophets results in their speaking, not from the Spirit per se, but more distinctively from God the Father.

The Son's role in sending the Spirit at Pentecost further supports this way of thinking. Recall with me Jesus's words to his disciples in John 16:12–15:

> I have many more things to say to you, but you cannot bear them now. But when He, the Spirit of truth, comes, He will

---

[18] Recall that at Constantinople (AD 381), the Cappadocian Fathers understood the Spirit's eternally "proceeding" from the Father as parallel, while not identical, to the Son's being eternally "begotten" by the Father. Both relations of origin (eternal begetting and eternal procession) imply the primacy of the Father, which then is reflected in the economic relations of the Father's "sending" and "speaking" through the Son and the Spirit.

guide you into all the truth; for He will not speak on His own initiative, but whatever He hears, He will speak; and He will disclose to you what is to come. He will glorify Me, for He will take of Mine and will disclose it to you. All things that the Father has are Mine; therefore I said that He takes of Mine and will disclose it to you.

(1) The Son speaks of the Spirit's relation to him much as he (the Son) had previously spoken of his relation with the Father. In John 8:28, Jesus states, "I do nothing on My own initiative, but I speak these things as the Father taught Me," but now, in John 16:14–15, Jesus says much the same of the Spirit. So the Spirit's relation to the Son parallels the Son's relation with the Father. Neither seeks to speak on his own initiative but speaks the word and accomplishes the work of another— the Son speaking and doing what the Father gives him, and the Spirit speaking and doing what the Son gives him.

Bear in mind how astonishing this is, that the Spirit, who has *not* become incarnate and so is exclusively and eternally God the Holy Spirit, submits to the will and word of the Son, who *is* incarnate when he makes this statement. We can account for this only as we understand the Spirit has always sought to assist the Son, and so has always been third among the trinitarian persons. The submission of the Spirit to the Son cannot be relegated to an "incarnational" expression (as some do in attempting to explain the submission of the Son). Rather the Spirit's speaking the word of the Father in submission to the Father (Heb 1:1) and teaching the word of the Son in submission to the Son (John 16:14–15) is the economic expression of his eternally proceeding from both the Father and the Son. Once again, eternal relations of origin ground the economic functional relation of authority and submission.

(2) John 16:15 adds another dimension that speaks directly to the question we are facing in Heb 1:1. While Jesus clearly declares that the Holy Spirit will speak of what the Son gives to him, what the

Son possesses and gives to the Spirit is not in fact his own. Rather, he (the Son) has received this from the Father. I find Jesus's words in John 16:15 nothing short of astonishing. After declaring so clearly and forcefully that the Spirit will not speak on his own but will speak the word the Son gives to him, Jesus immediately reminds his disciples of what he's told them before, that all he has is from the Father. The Son manifests a deep humility here, through his glad and willing recognition of the higher authority of the Father. So, indeed, the Spirit will speak the words that the Son gives him. However, since these words originate with the Father, the Spirit simultaneously speaks the words that the Father gives to him, mediated through the Son.

Hebrews 1:1 should be understood as indicating the ultimate source of what the prophets of old spoke to others: what they received was from the Father, so Hebrews can say the Father has spoken "long ago . . . in the prophets in many portions and many ways." This does not preclude the work of the Spirit, who as agent of the Father moves those very same prophets to speak what the Father, by the Spirit, inclines them to say (see again 2 Pet 1:21). In so doing, the prophets speak ultimately the word of the Father through Spirit-empowered human speech, so the Spirit is shown to be under the authority of the Father in a manner similar to the Son's place under the authority of the Father. The difference with the Spirit is this: whereas the Son is sent by the Father alone as under the authority of the Father alone, the Spirit is sent by the Father and the Son and so speaks and moves as the Son directs, reflecting the ultimate will and word of the Father.

Questions and Issues to Address

Although this is not the place for a full discussion of issues that come to the surface as one entertains the thesis of this chapter, some brief comments are appropriate.

(1) Issue: How can one uphold the inseparable operations that the pro-Nicene theologians found indispensable, along with the notion that the Father, Son, and Spirit each act in distinct ways as Scripture repeatedly indicates (e.g., Father sending, Son going, Spirit empowering)?

Response: I gladly affirm my commitment to the doctrine of the inseparable operations of the Father, Son, and Holy Spirit. Since each person of the Trinity possesses the identically same divine nature, each uses the same power and relies on the same knowledge and wisdom in conducting the various works that each does. So there cannot be a separation or division in the work of the one God, since each person participates fully in the one nature of God. However, this does not preclude each person accessing those qualities of the divine nature (e.g., power, knowledge, wisdom) distinctly yet harmoniously, according to their own hypostatic identity as Father, Son, or Holy Spirit, such that they bring to pass one unified result, accomplishing the one work of God. In this way, the personal works of the Father, Son, and Spirit may be distinct but never divided; each may focus on particular aspects of the divine work yet only together accomplish the one, harmonious, unified work of God. Each work of the trinitarian persons, then, is inseparable, while aspects of that one work are hypostatically distinguishable. Inseparable, but not indistinguishable—this accounts for the full biblical record of the works of God, which are unified works done by the one God, yet always carried out in hypostatically distinguishable ways.

Thomas McCall urged just such an understanding when he wrote, "Traditional trinitarian theology has stoutly insisted that the works of the triune persons are never *divided*; to the contrary, the works of the Trinity are 'always undivided' (*opera ad extra omnia sunt indivisa*)." But, he continues, this should not "be taken to imply that the agency of the divine persons in the economy is not genuinely distinct. . . . Anything less was seen as a kind of modalism and accordingly was labeled as a heresy. One of the Trinity suffered in the flesh. The work of the triune God 'outside of God' is always undivided, and in such a way that the divine persons operate distinctly in their relations to one another and to creation by the undivided divine power."[19]

Khaled Anatolios assists on this issue when discussing the position on divine agency advanced by Gregory of Nyssa. Anatolios writes that Gregory ruled out the notion of the trinitarian persons functioning as separate agents, working independently of one another. But, he continues,

> the notion of an altogether undifferentiated agency in which each of the persons partakes in exactly the same manner is also implicitly but very clearly ruled out by Gregory's consistent strategy of using three different verbs to distribute the common action distinctly to the three persons. . . . [T]he typical pattern for that distribution is that every action issues from the Father, is actualized through the Son, and is completed by the Spirit. There is thus an ineffable distinction within unity in divine co-activity such that the one divine activity is completely effected by each of the persons and yet is distinctly inflected between them. Every activity that is originated by the Father is equally yet distinctly owned by Son and Spirit.[20]

I affirm what Anatolios suggests, that we can understand trinitarian coagency neither as "altogether undifferentiated" nor as divided and independent. Rather, the Father, Son, and Spirit perform all divine action in an undivided yet distinct manner, an inseparable and hypostatically distinguishable manner.

---

[19] Thomas H. McCall, "Relational Trinity: Creedal Perspective," in *Two Views on the Doctrine of the Trinity*, ed. Jason S. Sexton (Grand Rapids, MI: Zondervan, 2014), 121–122.

[20] Khaled Anatolios, *Retrieving Nicaea: The Development and Meaning of Trinitarian Doctrine* (Grand Rapids, MI: Baker, 2011), 231.

(2) Issue: The next question, regarding the will of God as this pertains to the one and undivided divine nature and the three distinct persons, is closely related. Can there be a will of authority (from the Father) and a will of submission (from the Son) without conceiving of separate and separable divine wills? Can there be a unity of the one divine will while also affirming a distinction in just how that one will is expressed?

Response: My answer is yes, but the issue is not simple. I would suggest that we consider two factors. (1) First, we should affirm what the church fathers did, that "will" as a volitional capacity is a property of the divine nature. So, in this sense, each of the three persons possesses the identically same will, just as each of them possesses the identically same power, and knowledge, and holiness, and love. Yet, while each possesses the same volitional capacity, each can also make use of that volitional capacity in distinct yet unified ways, according to his distinct hypostatic identities and modes of subsistence. So, while the Father may access the common divine will to initiate, the Son may access the divine will to carry out (e.g., "from" the Father, "through" the Son)—as has often been affirmed in trinitarian doctrine following the pattern in Scripture itself (e.g., 1 Cor 8:6). Given this, one might even speak of one unified will of God, as the volitional capacity common to all three, along with three "inflections" of the unified divine will (borrowing Anatolios's wording). One could also speak of these as three hypostatically distinct expressions of that one divine will or even three distinguishable acts of willing, which together bring to light the fullness of that one unified will. All three expressions display the particular ways each divine person activates that common will from his particular personhood in distinct yet undivided personal action. This way of understanding the will of God—one volitional capacity of nature with distinct expressions or inflections of willing from each of the three divine persons—is akin to how we should understand, for example, the intratrinitarian love of God. Love is a quality or attribute of the divine nature; as such, it is common to the Father and the Son and the Holy Spirit. Yet the Father's expression of love for the Son is distinctly paternal, as the Son's expression of love for the Father is distinctly filial, and the Holy Spirit's expression of love for Father and Son is distinctly his own—one common attribute of love with three expressions or inflections of that capacity of love through each of the three trinitarian persons.

Apart from such a perspective, it is difficult to imagine how the three trinitarian persons share in intimate fellowship, love, communication, and mutual support. While there is one divine will, there must also be what Anatolios refers to as "distinct inflections of the one divine will belonging distinctly to the three *hypostaseis*,"[21] lest we propose, even unwittingly, some form of modalism or unitarianism. Terminology here is difficult, but if we are to undergird the genuineness of shared love and fellowship in the Trinity, and if we are to acknowledge the trinitarian grammar of divine willing that is expressed from the Father, through the Son, and completed by the Spirit, then something along the lines of one unified divine will of volitional capacity along with three distinct yet undivided inflections or expressions of willing by the three persons needs to be upheld. As a result, we can conceive, for example, how the Father can plan, purpose and will to send the Son (John 6:38; Eph 1:9; 1 John 4:10), and the Son accept and embrace the will of the Father (John 4:34). These are "distinct inflections" of the one and unified divine will, as seen from the particular hypostatic perspectives of the Father and the Son.

(2) Related to the above discussion and implied by it, we also affirm that the actual content or substance of the one divine will is shared fully by the Father, and by the Son, and by the Holy Spirit. So there never are three wills as if this expresses three different plans or purposes, each devised distinctly by the three persons and different in

---

[21] Anatolios, *Retrieving Nicaea*, 220 n. 234.

what they would seek to do. Rather, the will of the Father to send the Son is congruous with the will of the Son to go to earth, insofar as the very content of the divine will of both Father and Son is identically the same, namely, the will for the Son to go to earth to save sinners. But as we saw above, this does not rule out the hypostatically distinctive expressions of the one will, with the Father distinctly initiating the sending of the Son, and the Son distinctly embracing his coming to earth as the Father sends him. While the content of the one will is the same—go and save sinners—the expressions of that divine content are hypostatically distinctive.

(3) Issue: Is the Son free in his willing to obey the will of the Father? Some might think that if the Son must embrace the Father's will, then he cannot truly be free in accepting to do the Father's will. This issue is raised by Glenn Butner, who dismisses the notion that the Father could genuinely will in an authoritative way and the Son in a submissive way since the Son cannot will other than the Father has willed. He writes, "[T]he Son cannot submit to the Father because such submission requires freedom."[22]

Response: This objection stands only if the kind of freedom one is considering is libertarian freedom, the so-called power of contrary choice. That is, Butner's criticism works only if the freedom by which the Son is said to "freely obey" the Father is one in which he can equally obey or disobey the Father (i.e., the Son has libertarian freedom which requires the power of contrary choice). I have argued elsewhere that libertarian freedom is a failed concept that neither explains why moral agents choose precisely what they do nor accords with the strong sovereignty of God we see throughout the Scriptures.[23] If we adopt

---

[22] D. Glenn Butner Jr., "Eternal Functional Subordination and the Problem of the Divine Will," *JETS* 58, no. 1 (March 2015): 147.

[23] Bruce A. Ware, *God's Greater Glory: The Exalted God of Scripture and the Christian Faith* (Wheaton, IL: Crossway, 2004), 85–95; and "The Compatibility of Determinism and Human Freedom," in *Whomever He Wills: A Surprising Display of*

instead the concept of freedom in which our freedom consists in our unconstrained ability to do what we most want or to act according to our highest inclination—sometimes referred to as a "freedom of inclination"—then this problem is removed. The Son's willing submission is his free and unconstrained expression of what he most wants to do when he receives the authoritative will of the Father, which is always, without exception, to embrace and carry out precisely what the Father gives him to do.

(4) Issue: Have the proponents of ERAS (eternal relations of authority and submission among the trinitarian persons) denied the Nicene doctrine of the eternal generation of the Son?

Response: The answer emphatically, and for all proponents of our view whom I know, is no. We have never denied this doctrine, and indeed we affirm it as declaring very important truths about the eternal relation between the Father and the Son, the eternal deity and unity of both the Father and the Son, and the eternal fatherhood of the Father and eternal sonship of the Son.

Allow me to offer two reasons why I hold to both the eternal generation of the Son and the eternal procession of the Spirit: (1) I have great respect for the history of this doctrine, knowing its near-universal acceptance throughout the history of the church, and this provides strong reason to accept it as the heritage of the church to us now in the twenty-first century. Indeed, the church read the Johannine "begotten" language as indicating this doctrine, and it appears (as mentioned above) that the Fathers' understanding best reflects what John meant. The Fathers and nearly all who have followed them have seen the Bible teach the Son as eternally begotten from the Father; with this near uniform testimony, I gladly stand in this long tradition.[24] (2) Also

---

Sovereign Mercy, ed. Matthew M. Barrett and Thomas J. Nettles (Cape Coral, FL: Founders Press, 2012), 212–30.

[24] Full disclosure leads me to acknowledge that this does represent a change in my position. I have never in the past said that the doctrine of eternal

important to me is my long-standing commitment to what I see very clearly in the Bible, and that is the eternal fatherhood of the Father, and the eternal sonship of the Son. Just how is the one who is called "Father" in fact *eternal* Father, and just how is the one called "Son" in fact *eternal* Son? The doctrine of the eternal relations of origin offers the only real and available grounding for this truth. While the Father is eternal Father, and the Son the eternal Son, the best way to account for these truths is by affirming what the church has taught, that is, that the Father eternally begets the Son, and the Son is eternally begotten of the Father. As a result, I accept and embrace the doctrine of the eternal relations as the "church's doctrine" and the only genuine explanation that grounds the Father as eternal Father, and the Son as eternal Son.

Does affirming the eternal relations of origin or modes of subsistence cause problems for my commitment to an eternal relation of authority and submission in the Godhead? Absolutely not! It only strengthens the view. Precisely because the Father eternally begets the Son, the Father, as eternal Father of the Son, has the intrinsic paternal hypostatic property of having authority over his Son; and precisely because the Son is eternally begotten by the Father, the Son, as eternal Son of the Father, has the intrinsic filial hypostatic property of being in submission to his Father. The eternal relations of origin, then, ground the eternal distinction between Father and Son (and Spirit), such that the eternal relations of authority and submission naturally flow from and are expressive of those eternal relations of origin. Eternal (ontological) relations of origin and eternal (functional and hypostatic) relations of authority and submission work like hand and glove.

---

generation is wrong, but I have questioned whether Scripture teaches it, and frankly I've puzzled over just what it means. That I have now come to embrace this doctrine is evidence, to my way of thinking, of God's gracious continued work in my mind and heart, to move me closer to the truth of his word. For my previous position, see my *Father, Son, and Holy Spirit: Relationships, Roles, and Relevance* (Wheaton, IL: Crossway, 2005), 162 n. 3.

(5) Issue: Is it not the case that affirming the *eternal* authority of the Father over the Son, and the *eternal* submission of the Son to the Father, indicates both the superiority of the Father over the Son and that the Father has a different nature than the Son?

Response: No, neither of these problems follows. Allow me to address each separately. First, the Father's authority over the Son does not indicate he is superior to the Son because (1) the Father and the Son each possesses the identically same nature and hence both are absolutely coeternal and coequal in nature, and (2) authority and submission describe merely the manner in which these persons relate to each other, not what is true of the nature of the Father or the Son. In other words, authority and submission are functional and hypostatic, not essential (i.e., of the divine essence) or ontological categories, and hence they cannot rightly be invoked as a basis of declaring one person's ontology (nature) greater and the other's lesser. Ontologically the Father and Son are fully and identically equal, but, as persons, they function in an eternal Father-Son relation, in which the Father always acts in a way that befits who he is as Father, and the Son always acts in a way that befits who he is as Son. Their Father-Son manner of relating (functioning) is seen (in part) in the authority of the Father and submission of the Son, as is evidenced by the vast array of the biblical self-revelation of the trinitarian persons. And, since the Father is eternal Father, and the Son eternal Son, this manner of relating is likewise eternal.

Second, can the Father truly have the same nature as the Son when the Father has eternal authority over the Son? Yes, because "authority" and "submission" do not define or characterize the one and undivided nature that the Father and Son (and Spirit) share fully together, nor should they be thought of as attributes of God, per se. Holiness, wisdom, and power, of course, are attributes of God, and these (and all other) divine attributes are possessed equally and fully by the Father and the Son, since each possesses the same eternal and undivided divine nature. But authority and submission are ways of relating, not attributes of one's being. Put differently, authority and submission are hypostatic and functional properties pertaining to the persons in relation to one another, not ontological attributes attaching to the one commonly shared divine nature. That authority is a relational property and not an attribute of one's nature can be seen, for example, when Jesus says, "All authority in heaven and on earth has been given to me" (Matt 28:18 ESV; cf. Ps 2:8; Eph 1:22; Phil 2:8). Clearly, as authority is granted to him (by the Father, presumably), no addition to either his human or divine natures occurs. He had the same divine nature and the same human nature both before and after that authority was granted to him. Rather, he now has a relational property and functional position vis-à-vis the created order that he did not have previously. Or one might consider more simply a child who at one time is under authority (of his parents) but later, as an adult, exercises authority (over his children), and yet no change to his human nature takes place. The change occurs only in the manner of his relation to others. So, while the Father and Son are fully equal in nature, as each possesses the identically same and eternal divine nature, the Father and Son are also distinct persons, with person-specific properties that express the ways in which they eternally relate as Father to Son, and Son to Father, including hypostatically distinct paternal authority and hypostatically distinct filial submission.

(6) Issue: Must one hold that the relation of authority and submission between the Father and Son is, strictly speaking, eternal? Or might one satisfy the fullness of biblical teaching with the view that authority and submission began, if not in the incarnation, then in the forming of the covenant of redemption, the *pactum salutis*, when the plans and purposes for creation and redemption were settled? Must one hold the particular view proposed in the present chapter on the *eternal* relations of authority and submission among the members of the Trinity?

Response: Consider that the relation of authority and submission we see among the trinitarian persons is either eternal or it is not. The binary precision here is helpful; there is not a third option. If it is not eternal, then it starts. Binary again. And if it starts, one must inquire, just when, why, and how does it start? Some might say that it starts (and finishes) in the earthly life and ministry of Christ. Others might include also his submission to the Father in eternity future since the Son remains the incarnate Son forever. The main problem with both is the mountain of biblical evidence of the Father's role in planning, designing, sending, to be accomplished through the Son and Spirit, all of which takes place long before the incarnation, indeed long before creation, in what might be called eternity past (e.g., Eph 1:4–5, 9–11; 1 Pet 1:20). But should this be limited to the economic eternity past? If so, then this relation of authority and submission starts in the eternity past of the planning of the economy and is not, strictly speaking, absolutely eternal (i.e., not expressive of trinitarian relations *ad intra*, apart from creation).

But then one faces this very important question: why does the authority and submission relation in the economic eternity past take the precise shape that it does? That is, why is it that the one we call "Father" turns out to be the one who designs, plans, commands, and sends; and why is it that the one we call "Son" embraces, yields, obeys, and prepares to be sent? Is the assigning of authority and submission here in the economy to particular persons arbitrary and ad hoc such that it just so happened that the one we call "Father" is assigned authority, and the one we call "Son" is assigned submission, yet it may have been different? Could it have been that the one we call "Son" sends, and the one we call "Father" is sent to become incarnate? If not, just where would these expressions of authority and submission be rooted? Might it not rather be that there is no "assigning" of authority and submission at the point of the *pactum salutis* since authority and submission are embedded already (eternally) in the hypostatic identities of the divine persons?

Consider two helpful historical statements, the first from St. Augustine:

> The Son is not just said to have been sent because the Word became flesh, but that he was sent in order for the Word to become flesh, and by his bodily presence to do all that was written. That is, we should understand that it was not just the man who the Word became that was sent, but that the Word was sent to become man. For he was not sent in virtue of some disparity of power or substance or anything in him that was not equal to the Father, but in virtue of the Son being from the Father, not the Father being from the Son.[25]

A very important part of this quotation, for our purposes here, is Augustine's declaration that the Son was sent (in the economy) "in virtue of the Son being from the Father, not the Father being from the Son" (i.e., according to their eternal relations of origin or modes of subsistence). Thus the economic outworking reflects the immanent and eternal ontological relations such that it was not at all arbitrary that the Father is the one who sends the Son.

The words of Jonathan Edwards shine yet more light on our question:

> Though a subordination of the persons of the Trinity in their actings be not from any proper natural subjection one to another, and so must be conceived of as in some respect established by mutual free agreement . . . yet this agreement establishing this economy is not to be looked upon as merely arbitrary. . . . But there is a natural decency or fitness in that order and economy that is established. 'Tis fit that the order

---

[25] Augustine, *The Trinity*, trans. Edmund Hill, in vol. 5, *The Works of St. Augustine* (Brooklyn, NY: New City Press, 1991), 4.27.

of the acting of the persons of the Trinity should be agreeable to the order of their subsisting: that as the Father is first in the order of subsisting, so he should be first in the order of acting. . . . Therefore the persons of the Trinity all consent to this order, and establish it by agreement, as they all naturally delight in what is in itself fit, suitable and beautiful.[26]

While I embrace fully what Edwards says here, I am left with this nagging question: what is behind the notion of this "natural decency or fitness" in the order of authority and submission? What makes it decent and fit for the order to work out this way? His answer seems to be found in this claim: "'Tis fit that the order of the acting of the persons of the Trinity should be agreeable to the order of their subsisting." But then, if this is the case (i.e., if it is the case that the order of acting, which is worked out in a structure of authority and submission, is "agreeable" to the order of subsisting), then I cannot help but ask, could it really have worked out any other way? Does this not reflect, then, what necessarily must be the case when the economy of creation and redemption is devised, even though the trinitarian persons consent and delight in this order at the same time? It seems that the answer must be yes.

It follows that the relations of authority and submission evident in the economy *ad extra* are rooted in and are expressive of the eternal relations of origin within the Trinity *ad intra*. Stated differently, the Father possesses the personal property of paternal authority, as expressed in the economy, precisely because in the order of subsistence he is the unbegotten Father. The Son possesses the personal

---

[26] Jonathan Edwards, "Economy of the Trinity and Covenant of Redemption," in *The Works of Jonathan Edwards, vol. 20: The "Miscellanies," 833–1152*, ed. Amy Plantinga Pauw (New Haven, CT: Yale University Press, 2002), 1062, accessed April 1, 2016, http://edwards.yale.edu/archive?path=aHR0cDovL2Vkd2FyZH MueWFsZS5lZHUvY2dpLWJpbi9uZXdwaGlsby9nZXRvYmplY3QucGw/Yy4y4xOT ozOjIyNy53amVv#note1.

property of filial submission to the Father, as expressed in the economy, precisely because in the order of subsistence he is the begotten Son. Does this bring us to affirming that the relations of authority and submission among the trinitarian persons are strictly eternal, and not merely economic?

Some might quarrel: what you have shown is that economic authority and submission are rooted in and are expressive of the eternal modes of subsistence, but you have not shown that these relations are themselves eternal. Here is the rub. Are the relations of authority and submission evident in the economy expressive of those same relations among the persons of the immanent Trinity *ad intra*, or are they expressed only in the contingent economy *ad extra*?

In response, it is clear that we are approaching the point of sheer mystery in which we face limitations of what God has and has not revealed. God has not spoken to us about the inner trinitarian functional relations within the immanent Trinity, apart from creation. Presumably there are such functional relations apart from creation, since God is not static, yet we have not been told just what these are. Deuteronomy 29:29 reminds us there are innumerable "secret things," and this should sober us all in these pursuits. Even so, and with caution, I suggest there are problems in affirming *merely economic* and not also *eternal* relations of authority and submission, even when those relations are rooted in the eternal modes of subsistence.

One central difficulty is this: if what we see in the economy is not actually expressive of what is true in the immanent Trinity, then is what we call the self-revelation of God truly his *self*-revelation? Do we not ultimately face the possibility that God in himself is strikingly different from all that has been revealed to us regarding the trinitarian persons' relations and roles? In contrast, does it not stand to reason that what God has shown himself to be in the economy is himself? I cannot believe that God would bother to make so abundant and clear the nature of the trinitarian persons' relations and roles *ad extra*, but that none of this truly depicts God *ad intra*. This latter scenario might be likened to actors on a stage who purposely dress and act in ways that disguise their true off-stage identities, so that watching them perform on the stage gives us no real knowledge of who they truly are. The agnostic implications here are both sobering and unacceptable. If anything is clear in Scripture it is this: God has made himself known, and he calls us to cherish the truth that our eternal life is found in nothing less or other than in knowing him (Isa 11:9; Jer 9:23–24; Jer 31:31–34; John 17:3). Therefore, I'm far more inclined to think what God has shown us of himself is an outward and economic expression of who he truly is in himself.

The claim that an authority-submission relation among the trinitarian persons began at some point (e.g., with the *pactum salutis*, or in the incarnation) is just as much an epistemic claim to know something about the eternal relations among the trinitarian persons *ad intra* as that made by the advocates of ERAS. However, deniers of ERAS claim to know that there is *not* an eternal relation of authority and submission among the trinitarian persons in the immanent Trinity, and hence God eternally is *not* what he has revealed to us. But were one to claim that God actually is, from all eternity, different from what the entirety of his self-revelation in Scripture indicates, a very important question would then be, on what basis can one claim to know that God *actually is other than* the fullness of what his self-revelation has told us? Since all the self-revelation of God in Scripture indicates the eternality of the Father-Son relation flowing from the eternal relations of origin, along with the accompanying authority and submission structure evident from before the creation of the world, we simply have no grounds for ascertaining anything to the contrary. Instead, we have strong reason for concluding that the authority and submission structure we see everywhere in God's self-revelation in Scripture reflects the eternal ontological relations of origin. Here it seems, then, that the advocates of ERAS are on a stronger footing because they simply are claiming that God is as he has revealed himself—eternally and immutably.

A second difficulty arises when recognizing that the names "Father" and "Son" themselves lend support to seeing the relations of authority and submission as eternal and not merely economic. Father-son relationships are certainly characterized by far more than mere authority and submission, and we see this in the relation of the divine Father and divine Son. Their love, fellowship, harmony, and mutual glorification depict precious aspects of this Father-Son relationship, to be sure. But at the heart of the economy, it means that the Son gives full and joyful obedience to the Father. Jesus declares, for example, "I do as the Father has commanded me, so that the world may know that I love the Father" (John 14:31 ESV). Given how prominent this theme is in the economic outworking of their Father-Son relationship, do we really want to say that this has no place in their relationship in the immanent Trinity between the eternal Father and eternal Son? Again, I am far more inclined to believe that the Father and Son we see in the fullness of the economic revelation fundamentally depict, rather than distort, the eternal relation that is theirs.

It seems, then, that there is compelling basis for affirming that the authority and submission relations among the persons of the Trinity are eternal. At a minimum, we can say that the economic and contingent expression of this relation *ad extra* is rooted in and expressive of the eternal relations of origin *ad intra*. But beyond this, I argue that if the self-revelation of God truly is exactly that, the self-revelation *of God*, and if his Father-Son relation depicted in all that we see in Scripture truly describes that relation, then it follows that the relation of authority and submission in the Trinity is indeed eternal (i.e., eternal in the stronger, *ad intra*, sense of eternal). Because the Father is the eternal Father of the Son, in that he eternally begets the Son, the Father eternally acts in ways that befit who he is as Father, including, among other things, his eternal paternal authority. Because the Son is the eternal Son of the Father, in that he is eternally begotten by the Father, the Son eternally acts in ways that befit who he is as Son, including, among other things, his eternal filial submission. Because the Spirit is the eternal Spirit, in that he eternally proceeds from the Father and the Son, he eternally acts in ways that befit who he is as Spirit, including, among other things, his pneumatic assistance to the Son in his submission to the Father. In the end, I think that J. I. Packer, more than forty years ago, got it exactly right:

> Part of the revealed mystery of the Godhead is that the three Persons stand in a fixed relation to each other. . . . It is the nature of the second person of the Trinity to acknowledge the authority and submit to the good pleasure of the first. That is why he declares himself to be the Son and the first person to be his Father. Though coequal with the Father in eternity, power and glory, it is natural to him to play the Son's part and to find all his joy in doing his Father's will, just as it is natural to the first person of the Trinity to plan and initiate the works of the Godhead and natural to the third person to proceed from the Father and the Son to do their joint bidding. Thus the obedience of the God-man to the Father while he was on earth was not a new relationship occasioned by the Incarnation, but the continuation in time of the eternal relationship between the Son and the Father in heaven.[27]

Conclusion

Within the relations and roles of the Father, the Son, and the Spirit, one finds a prevailing authority and submission structure that flows from the eternal relations of origin and gives order and direction to the ways the three trinitarian persons relate and function. This claim finds wide and uniform biblical support. While the Father is the planner, designer, originator, and instigator of divine activity (e.g., Eph

---

[27] J. I. Packer, *Knowing God* (Downers Grove, IL: InterVarsity, 1993; first published 1973), 54–55.

1:9–11), the Son and Spirit are agents of the Father who work unitedly to bring to pass what the Father has ordained (e.g., John 6:38; 15:26). While one finds the Father sending and commanding the Son and the Spirit, one does not find the Son commanding the Father or the Spirit sending the Father. These irreversible relations—the functional outworking of the eternal relations of origin that identify each person distinctively—give rise to consistent and eternal functional relations that Scripture testifies to repeatedly, relations that include the paternal authority of the eternal Father and filial submission of the eternal Son.

We have every reason to think that the eternal triune God is the same immanently as he is economically in this respect: God is eternally God only as he is unbegotten Father, begotten Son, and proceeding Holy Spirit. The Father, Son, and Spirit constitute the one God; as Father, Son, and Spirit they are also distinct persons whose roles reflect the eternal relations which are theirs. Authority and submission within the Godhead, then, are best understood as the expression of just how Father, Son, and Spirit relate in the created order, reflecting who they really and perfectly are in eternity. In faithfulness to the self-revelation of God, let us see more clearly the beauty of God's triune being, both in the equality and in the distinctiveness of the trinitarian persons, and may this lead us to greater worship of and devotion to the one God who is three.

CHAPTER 2

From God to Humanity: A Trinitarian Method for Theological Anthropology

By Malcolm B. Yarnell III

After completing the text now published under the title, *God the Trinity: Biblical Portraits,* I was approached by the editor of this volume to participate in an interesting dialogue with leading evangelical Baptist theologians. This essay is the result of that discussion, which focused on the theological method behind our trinitarian anthropology. As that conversation and this resulting text demonstrate, attempting to construct a theological anthropology presents us with methodological difficulties. These challenges profoundly impact how one theologically conceives of both the Creator God and creaturely humanity.

The following essay outlines my own theological method for the purpose of providing a description of human beings in relation to God and in relation to one another, with particular concern for the male relation with the female. The method is fourfold: First, I argue that consideration of the doctrine of God must precede the doctrine of humanity. Second, I affirm that God reveals himself in a realistic manner. Third, I demonstrate that God's self-revelation is uniquely located in the persons of the Father, the Son, and the Holy Spirit. Finally, I argue that humanity has been created (and is being re-created) in the image of this God who is Trinity.

From Theology Proper to Theological Anthropology

One's starting place when addressing the relationship between theology proper, the doctrine of God, theological anthropology, and the doctrine of humanity sets the crucial methodological direction. It could be argued that because the entire canon of Christian Scripture begins with the presupposition of God as the subject who acts in creating (Gen 1:1) and only subsequently addresses the divine creation of humanity (Gen 1:26), we must likewise prioritize the doctrine of God over the doctrine of humanity. If the theologian allows the literary discourse of divine revelation to establish his method, the doctrine of God both precedes and grounds the doctrine of humanity. However, the literary priority of every biblical book does not follow this theological priority. Herod, Zechariah, and Elizabeth (Luke 1:5) appear in Luke's Gospel prior to the first reference to God (1:6). But this literary construction by no means indicates that Luke gave theological priority to those three human characters in his Gospel narrative. Furthermore, the revelation of certain propositional truths in the canon (while contextually revealed) provides the basis for granting the doctrine of God methodological priority in the systematic relationship between Christian doctrines.

The progression of the creation narrative grounds anthropology in the doctrine of God, culminating with the creation of humanity in the divine likeness and image. According to Gen 1:26–27, humanity was created in the "image" (*selem*) and "likeness" (*demuth*) of God, and not vice versa. Two propositions supporting the priority of God arise from these verses. First is the proposition that humanity is reflective of God. Man (*adam*)—humanity as inclusive of male (*zakar*) and female (*neqebah*)—being created in God's image and likeness indicates gendered humanity's derivative status. Theologians have sometimes looked inward toward humanity as a way of looking upward toward God, and this epistemological movement from humanity to God is typically based on the prior claim that humanity is made to image the divine, not vice versa. One may derivatively perceive God in humanity, because humanity is made to reflect God.

The second, and related, proposition supporting the priority of God states that God is the Creator of humanity. The causal movement from Creator to creature indicates the priority of the being of God in relation to the being of humanity. On the basis of these two propositional claims, along with the literary priority of the doctrine of God within the progress of the Genesis narrative, I believe that theology proper ought to precede and ground theological anthropology. Thus I will argue that one should look primarily to who God is before reflecting on who humanity is. I agree with Michael Allen when he says, "Theology follows the biblical order itself: God, then all other things as they play out in redemptive history."[1]

Not every theologian, however, has followed this method. For instance, Augustine's method in the latter part of his famous *De Trinitate* was to approach God as Trinity through an examination of individual human psychology.[2] Likewise, Augustine's treatment of God as Creator appeared in three books of his even more famous *Confessions*, but only after an intensive and prayerful evaluation of his human self in the first

---

[1] Michael Allen, "Knowledge of God," in *Christian Dogmatics: Reformed Theology for the Church Catholic*, ed. Michael Allen and Scott R. Swain (Grand Rapids: Baker Academic, 2016), 26.

[2] Augustine, *De Trinitate*, bks. 9–15.

ten books.[3] Within the stream of Western Christianity, whose entire
course flows inevitably through the straits of Augustine, there is ample
precedent for treating man before God. While Augustine's method is
by no means out of bounds, it does grant an undeniably solipsistic tendency to his theological anthropology.[4] One way that Augustine over-
comes the individualist anthropocentrism of his theological method
is through elevating divine fiat in his account of salvation.[5] I prefer to
mitigate the problems inherent within Augustinian anthropology and
soteriology by prioritizing theology before anthropology.

For others, such as John Calvin, theological truth arises not through
prioritizing God or humanity, but in an epistemological dialectic
between God and man: one comes to know both God's self and the
human self through increasing in knowledge of both.[6] Calvin's order
has some natural appeal, because it reminds us of man's fallen nature
and God's eminent majesty, and because it correlates with human
experience in coming to know God. I believe that Calvin's theological
method is preferable to Augustine's, because it more readily gives God
the position of priority. Moreover, Calvin's method is helpful because,

---

[3] For a recent illuminating review of Augustine's *Confessions* from a classical literary and philosophical perspective, see Robin Lane Fox, *Augustine:
Conversions to Confessions* (New York: Basic Books, 2015). The best historical and
theological review remains Peter Brown, *Augustine of Hippo: A Biography*, new ed.
(Berkeley, CA: University of California Press, 2000).

[4] We might even cheekily argue that Augustine's theological method historically encourages an anthropological theology, but we do not have space here
to advance that argument.

[5] Providing a theological account of human salvation is the burden of Augus-
tine's attacks on the Pelagians. See, in particular, Augustine, *On the Spirit and
the Letter*, *On Nature and Grace*, and *On Grace and Free Will*, in *Augustine: Anti-
Pelagian Writings*, trans. Peter Holmes, Robert Ernest Wallis, and Benjamin B.
Warfield, Nicene and Post-Nicene Fathers, 1st series, vol. 5 (reprint, Peabody,
MA: Hendrickson, 1994), 80–115, 116–54, and 436–67.

[6] John Calvin, *Institutes of the Christian Religion*, ed. John T. McNeill, trans.
Ford Lewis Battles, Library of Christian Classics, vol. 20 (Philadelphia:
Westminster Press, 1960), 1.1.1–3.

as theologians and philosophers have long recognized, human beings may speak of God only through the use of human language. Even if we wished to begin with God ontologically, we must deal with humanity simultaneously through the necessary instrument of our knowledge, the gift of human language.

Traditionally, theologians have appealed to categories that help the human being recognize the utility and limitations of human language. They have brought forward such ideas as that God has *accommodated* himself to humanity through the created gift of language and the revealed gift of his own name. Moreover, human beings have learned to ascribe meaning to the name of God through their covenantal experience with him.[7] Of course, the simultaneous utility and limitations of language have prompted theologians and philosophers to categorize most speech about God as neither *univocal* nor *equivocal*, but *analogical*.[8] To say that we can speak of God by analogy indicates that theological words tell us something true about God, even as these human terms still do not fully convey him.

Another means by which theologians have categorized language about God is through the three ways of construing knowledge of God: *via causalitatis*, *via negativa*, and *via eminentiae*. *Via causalitatis* is the positive way of speaking about God and involves working from a created effect back to the divine cause. It appeals to such positive junctions between human experience and divine reality as the confession about God found in Exod 34:6: "The LORD—the LORD is a compassionate and gracious God, slow to anger and abounding in faithful love and truth" (CSB). *Via negativa*, the negative way of speaking about God, denies there is a correlation between God and the human

---

[7] Helpful in this regard is Stanley Grenz, *The Named God and the Question of Being: A Trinitarian Theo-Ontology* (Louisville, KY: Westminster John Knox, 2005), 250–90.

[8] For a summary description of these three terms from Aquinas, see John H. Hick, *Philosophy of Religion*, 4th ed. (Englewood Cliffs, NJ: Prentice-Hall, 1990), 83–85.

idea. It appeals to such disjunctions between God and humanity as found in Num 23:19: "God is not a man, that he should lie, or a son of man, that he should change his mind" (ESV).[9] The third way, *via eminentiae*, operates between the positive and negative ways of speaking about God. The eminent way affirms that we may speak of God but not with fullness of knowledge and only as the result of God's revelation of himself. It says that we may begin with a human definition but must recognize that God excels all such human descriptions.[10]

Now that we've stated the conviction that theology precedes anthropology, even as we acknowledge that revealed language about God is still human, we turn to describe the theological method that leads us to move from theological reflection on God to theological reflection on man, and even beyond into ethics. The priority of theology and the necessity of human dependence on divine revelation, a revelation that uses human language, calls for three affirmations. First, God is who he reveals himself to be. Second, God reveals himself to be Father, Son, and Holy Spirit. Third, humanity is created (and is being re-created) in the image of the Trinity. The first statement calls for further exploration into the doctrine of revelation, the second into the doctrine of God, and the third brings us to the doctrine of humanity.

God Is Who He Reveals Himself to Be

Many biblical texts could be used to demonstrate the truth of our second claim. We turn to a conversation in John 14:8–11. Interrupting his master's doctrinal discourse, Philip said to Jesus, "Lord . . . show us the Father, and that's enough for us." Jesus said to him, "Have I been

---

[9] *Via causalitatis* is also called the "cataphatic" approach, and *via negativa* is also known as the "apophatic" approach.

[10] See Emil Brunner, *The Christian Doctrine of God*, trans. Olive Wyon, *Dogmatics*, vol. 2 (Philadelphia: Westminster Press, 1946), 245–46.

among you all this time and you do not know me, Philip? The one who has seen me has seen the Father." A little later, Jesus added two further relevant statements: "Don't you believe that I am in the Father and the Father is in me?" and "The words I speak to you I do not speak on my own. The Father who lives in me does his works" (CSB). While Philip sensed that he lacked only the revelation of God the Father to fulfill his existence, Jesus indicated the revelation of the Father was immediately available to him, visibly present before him. The revelation of the invisible God is the visible man Jesus. There is a threefold truth to be garnered from this exchange about the revelation of God.

First, there is a correlation between Jesus and the Father: "The one who has seen me has seen the Father" (CSB). Philip did not see what was before him; the revelation of God is the Son. Second, there is a distinction between Jesus and the Father: "The words I speak to you I do not speak on my own. The Father who lives in me does his works" (CSB). While he is the revelation of the Father, Jesus is clearly distinguished from the Father. The words that Jesus speaks are a work of the Father. The words are conveyed through the Son but originate with the Father. The third truth from this dialogue indicates that the relation between Jesus and the Father is one of unparalleled intimacy, a mutual indwelling. This third truth is stated in a chiastic parallel: "I am in the Father and the Father is in me" (14:10a CSB); and "I am in the Father and the Father is in me" (14:11a CSB). The revelation of God begins in the shared existence of Father and Son with the Father as the originating source; it continues with the Son as the instrumental source; it concludes as God presents himself to a human being, Philip. The failure of Philip to receive this gift of knowledge does not detract from the revelation of the divine reality.

Moisés Silva perceives a similar correspondence between divine reality and that reality's availability to humanity through divine revelation. He draws out this correspondence in his exegesis of the noun ἀλήθεια ("truth" or "truthfulness") and its cognate adjective ἀληθινός ("real" or "true") in John's Gospel. For instance, John 1:14 builds on the request of Moses to see God in Exodus 33–34. Where Moses was only granted hindsight of God, Jesus is himself the full revelation of God. Citing Rudolf Schnackenberg, Silva says that in Christ, "divine reality" is accessible "in a more strongly ontological sense."[11] John writes elsewhere that the truth is opposed to falsehood, provides a valid witness, differs from mere appearance, may be performed as well as known, and finds its personal antithesis in the devil.[12] From a trinitarian perspective, the truth is also directly identified with Jesus (John 14:6) and the Word (17:17), with the Father (17:3), and with the Holy Spirit (14:17; 15:26; 16:13).

From scriptural assertions like these, our epistemological conclusion is that a "realist conception of revelation" provides the best interpretation of human access to knowledge of God.[13] In other words, there is a truthful correspondence between divine revelation and human access to divine reality. The claim I am making has not gone without detractors in Christian history. In perhaps his finest contribution to academic theology, the late Stanley Grenz constructed a brilliant history of the arguments concerning human knowledge of divine ontology. Among those who helped bring about the demise of a realist perspective on human access to divine ontology were philosophers and theologians such as William of Ockham, Nicholas of Cusa, Isaac Newton, John Locke, David Hume, Immanuel Kant, Arthur Schopenhauer, and Jacques Derrida. On the other hand, there has been a substantive effort to retain a correspondence between ontology

---

[11] Moisés Silva, ed., *New International Dictionary of New Testament Theology and Exegesis*, 2nd ed., 5 vols. (Grand Rapids: Zondervan, 2014), 1:236.

[12] Silva, 1:231–40. Similar ideas are evident in the Pauline corpus, where the idea that the gospel is the truth is also prominent.

[13] Sebastian Rehnman provides a helpful review of such a revelation-oriented epistemological realism. Sebastian Rehnman, "A Realist Conception of Revelation," in *The Trustworthiness of God: Perspectives on the Nature of Scripture*, ed. Paul Helm and Carl R. Trueman (Grand Rapids: Eerdmans, 2002), 253–72.

and theology on the part of various realists, including Augustine of
Hippo, Thomas Aquinas, Jonathan Edwards, Georg Hegel, and Alfred
North Whitehead.[14]

Others whom we could add to Grenz's prestigious list of theological realists include John Wyclif, Dietrich Bonhoeffer, and Karl Rahner.
I have considered Wyclif and Rahner elsewhere,[15] so I will summarize Bonhoeffer's contribution here. André Dumas discerns within
the German martyr's tragically shortened, yet profoundly influential,
career a continual interest in human access to knowledge of divine reality. Bonhoeffer used three "conceptual approaches" to move toward
a Christological form of critical realism: "in *Act and Being* (1929) it
was ontology; in *Christ the Center* (1932) it was structuralism; and in
Ethics (1940–43) it was reality."[16] According to Dumas, Bonhoeffer was
continuing the long theological tradition of realism against challenges
from both Karl Barth and Rudolf Bultmann. Dumas helpfully summarizes the realist tradition's definition of *theology*: "It says two things:
(1) 'God is' and (2) 'I can speak of him,' and it implies that the conjunction 'and' does not create a gulf but an equivalence, or at least a
correlation."[17] If we turn to the final stage of Bonhoeffer's career, in his
writings on ethics, which were composed shortly before his death, we
find Bonhoeffer fully defending a realist approach to our knowledge
of God. Kant, the northern German sage of Königsberg, built the modern wall between humanity and humanity's knowledge of God. Barth,

---

[14] Grenz, *The Named God and the Question of Being*, 15–130.

[15] Malcolm B. Yarnell III, "John Wyclif's Universalist Approach to Universal
Priesthood," in *Royal Priesthood in the English Reformation* (New York: Oxford
University Press, 2013), 17–40; Malcolm B. Yarnell III, *God the Trinity: Biblical
Portraits* (Nashville, TN: B&H Academic, 2016), 164–76.

[16] André Dumas, *Dietrich Bonhoeffer: Theologian of Reality*, trans. Robert
McAfee Brown (London: SCM Press, 1971), 115. A similar chronological structure for evaluating Bonhoeffer's doctrine of Christ as place may be found in
Madison Grace, "The Church as Place in Dietrich Bonhoeffer's Theology" (PhD
diss., Southwestern Baptist Theological Seminary, 2012).

[17] Dumas, *Dietrich Bonhoeffer*, 5.

the southern German theologian of Basel, partially deconstructed it through his radical doctrine of transcendence, and Bonhoeffer, the central German theologian from Berlin, obliterated what remained. Bonhoeffer destroyed the wall using a Christological doctrine that correlates well with the teaching of Jesus in John 14. For Bonhoeffer, Jesus is the *sui generis* reality of God revealed.

Bonhoeffer unveils a threefold definition of how knowledge of divine reality proceeds from God to humanity.[18] First, Bonhoeffer denies the false claim that either the self or the world is the ultimate reality. He sternly asserts, "God alone is the ultimate reality."[19] Second, Bonhoeffer affirms that God reveals his reality to humanity only through Jesus Christ. He noticeably brings the revelation of God in Jesus Christ and the reality of God into an equivalent relation. "[T]he ultimate reality is revelation, that is, the self-witness of the living God."[20] Third, Bonhoeffer affirms that our access to knowledge of this reality is entirely dependent on God's self-revelation, Jesus Christ. Bonhoeffer expresses this from an ethical perspective, "[T]he decision about the whole of life depends on our relation to God's revelation."[21] Bonhoeffer encapsulates his realist doctrine of revelation in one sentence: "It is the reality of God that is revealed in Jesus Christ."[22]

In protest against those dualisms that posit a metaphysical gap between the world and God, Bonhoeffer argues that when humans speak of reality (or ontology or structure) they must embrace only one reality, *Christuswirklichkeit*, Christ-reality. There is simply no way

---

[18] I would be remiss not to give credit to my wife, Karen, whose personal reading notes on *Ethics* have insightfully shaped my understanding of Bonhoeffer here.

[19] Dietrich Bonhoeffer, "Christ, Reality, and Good: Christ, Church, and World," in *Dietrich Bonhoeffer Works*, ed. Clifford J. Green, trans. Reinhard Krauss, Charles C. West, and Douglas W. Stott, vol. 6, *Ethics* (Minneapolis: Fortress, 2005), 48.

[20] Bonhoeffer, 48.

[21] Bonhoeffer, 49.

[22] Bonhoeffer, 48.

for human beings to have access to any reality other than the reality of the world that has been created through, in, and for Jesus Christ. Bonhoeffer effectively excludes all nonrealist epistemologies from consideration:

> There are not two realities but *only one reality*, and that is God's reality revealed in Christ in the reality of the world. Partaking in Christ, we stand at the same time in the reality of God and in the reality of the world. The reality of Christ embraces the reality of the world in itself. The world has no reality of its own independent of God's revelation in Christ. . . . Hence there are not two realms, but only *the realm of the Christ-reality* [*Christuswirklichkeit*], in which the reality of God and the reality of the world are united.[23]

Dumas's summary of similar statements in the Bonhoeffer corpus is instructive: "Christ may be known as the present Christ who assures God's presence to reality and reality's presence before God."[24] Thanks to Bonhoeffer and other like-minded realist theologians, we may conclude that God is who he reveals himself to be. Moreover, the divine reality is revealed in and through Jesus Christ. In Christ (and we would add, by the Spirit), there is no gap between divine reality and divine revelation, even if our perception of that reality is corrupted through sin. Jesus's revelation of God's reality is true and trustworthy, whether Philip saw that reality or not.

God Reveals Himself to Be Father, Son, and Holy Spirit

After establishing from Scripture that God, through revelation, can tell us something important about God's own self, we may now examine exactly what that something is. What is revelation telling us about the

---

[23] Bonhoeffer, 58.

[24] Dumas, *Dietrich Bonhoeffer*, 116.

reality of God? What does God reveal about his eternal being, about his trinitarian ontology? While appreciative of the contributions of the great tradition of the universal church, I focus in this section on three recent presentations of what God reveals himself to be. These three affirmations of inner-trinitarian reality arose within North American evangelicalism, but each theologian is conversant with both the historical legacy and the recent ecumenical discussions. These three evangelicals have discerned within biblical revelation and in Christian history a certain dynamic of being within God as Trinity.

Stanley Grenz

The first author, Stanley J. Grenz, showed increasing concern with God as Trinity until his relatively early death in 2005, soon after his fifty-fifth birthday. The last three volumes that he contributed to contemporary systematic theology focused almost entirely on the Trinity, starting with trinitarian anthropology but with increasing concern for divine ontology. In *Rediscovering the Triune God*, Grenz summarized trinitarian theology from Karl Barth and Karl Rahner to his own day.[25] The other writings were the first two volumes in a proposed (but sadly incomplete) six-volume systematic theology titled *The Matrix of Christian Theology*. The first volume of the series, *The Social God and the Relational Self*, sought to construct a trinitarian basis for humanity as *imago Dei*.[26] The second volume, *The Named God and the Question of Being*, reconnected the link between theology and ontology, proposing a "theo-ontology" in place of the historically debased "onto-theology."[27]

---

[25] Stanley J. Grenz, *Rediscovering the Triune God: The Trinity in Contemporary Theology* (Philadelphia: Augsburg Fortress, 2004).

[26] Stanley J. Grenz, *The Social God and the Relational Self: A Trinitarian Theology of the Imago Dei* (Louisville, KY: Westminster John Knox, 2001).

[27] Stanley J. Grenz, *The Named God and the Question of Being: A Trinitarian Theo-Ontology* (Louisville, KY: Westminster John Knox, 2005).

In a most interesting twist, Grenz ended his career with a subtle and significant contribution to a contemporary biblical theology of the Trinity, alongside an appreciative review of the classical Christian discussion of trinitarian ontology.[28] In this final developed stage of trinitarian ontology, Grenz takes his reader through three sagas. In the first, as mentioned above, Grenz discerns a philosophical and theological movement into and out of what he calls "onto-theology." In the second saga, he builds the case from the biblical canon for what he calls a "theo-ontology."[29] Grenz observes within Exod 3:14 God's revelation of his being through a definite yet ambiguous self-naming as the singular "I am" (יהוה; transliterated as YHWH). God continued to add complexity to his revelation of himself in "the name" throughout the biblical canon, significantly with the Johannine ascriptions of "I am" to Jesus Christ. Grenz also discerns scriptural affirmations regarding the deity of the Holy Spirit.

From the third saga, Grenz concludes that with the correlation of the singular "name" in the Matthean baptismal formula, God's self-revelation reaches a high point. "In short, the saga of the I AM is ultimately the narrative of 'the Father and the Son and the Holy Spirit.' The saga of the divine name, in other words, is the saga of the relationships among the three persons of the Trinity."[30] So then, the relations within the Trinity define divine ontology. Grenz goes on to note that the exact structure of the Trinity's reality as Father, Son, and

---

[28] Heinrich Kehler wrote his dissertation on the trinitarian theology of Stanley Grenz, and his contributions have been instrumental toward my own understanding of Grenz's trinitarianism. See Heinrich Kehler, "The Social Trinitarian Doctrine of Stanley J. Grenz: A Unique, Albeit Questionable Result of His Theological Journey" (PhD diss., Southwestern Baptist Theological Seminary, 2016). See also Jason S. Sexton, *The Trinitarian Theology of Stanley J. Grenz* (New York: T&T Clark, 2015); Derek J. Tidball, Brian S. Harris, and Jason S. Sexton, eds., *Revisioning, Renewing, Rediscovering the Triune Center: Essays in Honor of Stanley J. Grenz* (Eugene, OR: Cascade, 2014).

[29] Grenz, *The Named God and the Question of Being*, 131–236.

[30] Grenz, 270.

Holy Spirit has been a point of contention, even among those who are
advocates of Nicene orthodoxy.

While he is adamant that the Trinity's internal structure is dynamic
rather than static, he does not alienate the more vertical Eastern view
from the more horizontal Western view. Grenz does prefer the "horizontal" Western noetic model.[31] Grenz embraces the internal dynamism emphasized with Augustine's model of divine love and offers
his own model of self-naming.[32] Even then, Grenz is careful to call on
the Cappadocians to provide a necessary "corrective" to the horizontal
model by recalling the otherness between the three.[33]

Scott Swain

Our second author, Scott R. Swain, has contributed works evaluating
the biblical evidence supporting the doctrine of the Trinity,[34] trinitarian hermeneutical method,[35] and systematic discourse concerning the
Trinity.[36] This academic leader's most recent effort is a concise and ele-
gant contribution to a broadly based Reformed systematic theology.[37]

---

[31] Grenz, 309. The Latin Christian theologian Marius Victorinus borrowed
this model from the Neo-Platonist philosopher, Plotinus. Augustine also seems
to have adapted it for his own use.

[32] Grenz, 334–40.

[33] Grenz, 338.

[34] Andreas J. Köstenberger and Scott Swain, *Father, Son and Spirit: The Trinity
and John's Gospel*, New Studies in Biblical Theology, vol. 24 (Downers Grove, IL:
InterVarsity Press, 2008).

[35] Scott R. Swain, *Trinity, Revelation, and Reading: A Theological Introduction to
the Bible and Its Interpretation* (New York: T&T Clark, 2011).

[36] Scott R. Swain, *The God of the Gospel: Robert Jenson's Trinitarian Theology*
(Downers Grove, IL: InterVarsity Press, 2013).

[37] Scott R. Swain, "Divine Trinity," in *Christian Dogmatics: Reformed Theology for
the Church Catholic*, ed. Michael Allen and Scott R. Swain (Grand Rapids: Baker
Academic, 2016), 78–106; see Swain, "The Covenant of Redemption," in Allen
and Swain, *Christian Dogmatics*, 107–25.

Regarding divine ontology, Swain begins with a similar identification between the divine "name" of God in Exod 3:14 and the New Testament Trinity. Like Grenz, Swain emphasizes the divine unity first through God's "proper name." "The identification of God by his proper name and its 'corona of connotation' reveals that YHWH is *one* and serves to indicate *what sort of one* he is."[38] The other gods will disappear before the truth that Yahweh is the only true God. This Old Testament characterization of Yahweh as the one true God continues in the New Testament as the New Testament uses the Septuagint's "standard 'surrogate' for God's proper name."[39] Yahweh's surrogate name in the Greek Old Testament and the Greek New Testament is κύριος, "the Lord." Yet mere unity is not what Swain has in mind: "We do not exhaust the significance of the name into which we are baptized by noting its singularity."[40] Like Grenz, Swain believes the singular name is expansive enough to include three. And these three are "personal names."

It is in his discussion of the personal names that Swain begins to tread a path ever more certainly away from Grenz. Where Grenz was reluctant to follow too far the more vertical model of the Cappadocians, Swain tracks more closely with these Eastern Nicene fathers. Drawing on swift but sure-footed biblical exegesis, Swain demonstrates that the personal names differentiate the three persons: "Unlike the Tetragrammaton, which signifies that which they hold in common, the personal names signify that which distinguishes the three from one another within the singular being of God."[41] According to Swain, the personal names indicate "relations of origin." These relations of origin enclose two ontological tendencies, toward correspondence and toward order. First, the New Testament patterns of the relation

[38] Swain, "Divine Trinity," 85.
[39] Swain, 86.
[40] Swain, 85.
[41] Swain, 87.

between the Father and the Son specify an "ontological correspondence between the Father and the Son." Second, this ontological correspondence "obtains within the context of a relationship wherein the
Father is the principle or source."[42]

Swain discerns a similar set of tendencies in the New Testament
with regard to the Holy Spirit. Distinct from the Father-Son relation,
which entails one person being the source of the other, Swain says
that both the Father and the Son serve as the economic source of the
Holy Spirit. Swain later adds that the Father and the Son are together,
not only the economic source, but also the ontological source of the
Holy Spirit. Swain avers, "The procession of the Spirit flows from two
persons rather than from one, albeit as from one spirating principle."[43]
He retains the Western double procession, approving the formulation
of Francis Turretin. The great Protestant scholastic theologian argued
that the double sending, an economic movement, implies a double
procession, an ontological movement: "temporal procession presup-
poses an eternal."[44] In this way, Swain holds to a more vertical model
than Grenz, but in an unmistakably Western form.

Also in a Western frame, Swain follows Augustine in adopting
two of Aristotle's ten categories of predication with regard to God.
The personal names of the three persons indicate "relational predication," because they have "reference to someone else," while the
Tetragrammaton indicates a "substantial predication," because it is
spoken "with reference to [God] himself."[45] Each of the three persons has a personal name that connotes a "personal property" that
is incommunicable to the other persons, even as all three share in
the divine substance. First, "[t]he personal property of the Father is

---

[42] Swain, 88–89.
[43] Swain, 89.
[44] Swain, "Divine Trinity," 101–2.
[45] Swain, 95. Cf. Mark Weedman, "Augustine's *De Trinitate* 5 and the Problem
of the Divine Names 'Father' and 'Son,'" *Theological Studies* 72 (2011): 768–86.

paternity," and with the Son, the Father also shares "the characteristic of spiration."[46] Second, "[t]he personal property of the Son is filiation or generation." The generation of the Son from the Father as source is an eternal movement, is not to be confused with creation, and occurs without division of the divine being.[47] Third, "[t]he personal property of the Spirit is procession."[48]

Malcolm Yarnell

Since we have been asked to describe our own trinitarian anthropological method, I will serve as the third evangelical in this conversation about trinitarian ontology. In dialogue with Grenz and Swain, it will become clear how my methodology is situated in relation to them. In the text of *God the Trinity*, I presented ten theses reflecting upon the nature of the Trinity. The first of these four theses focused on trinitarian ontology and will prove helpful in dialogue with the previous two authors.

First, I concluded that eight central canonical texts (Matt 28:19; 2 Cor 13:14; Deut 6:4–7a; John 1:18; 16:14–15; 17:21–22; Eph 1:3–14; Rev 5:6) teach the importance of creation's unique devotion to God. Like our two interlocutors, I discovered a unity within God that may not be compromised. There is one God, and he must be "radically differentiated" from creation. However, this is not a substance-oriented monotheism but a devotion-oriented monotheism. In concession to the usefulness of the philosophical tradition which Grenz and Swain both accept, I am not personally averse to the language of essence, substance, nature, being, ontology, or reality. From a devotional perspective, I concluded, "the simplicity of God encloses the Son and the Holy Spirit with the Father."[49] Finally, like Grenz, I would want to add

---

[46] Swain, "Divine Trinity," 99.

[47] Swain, 100.

[48] Swain, 101.

[49] Yarnell, *God the Trinity*, 228.

that any appropriation of the language of ontology should not be seen as compromising the eternal dynamism of God.

Second, we affirmed that there is a "threefold set of relations" in God. These relations are eternal realities affiliated with the "proper names" of the Father, the Son, and the Holy Spirit. Once again, I affirm both Grenz and Swain. However, I attach a different importance to the names. While other trinitarian theologians such as Kendall Soulen discuss the ideas indicated in naming,[50] Grenz broke new ground in *The Named God and the Question of Being*. There, he argued for a difference between naming as denotation and naming as connotation. The idea of naming as mere denotation says that proper names provide a "direct reference" to differentiate this subject from all others. The idea of naming as connotation says that proper names are "descriptivist" in the sense that they convey the object's nature to some extent.[51] Grenz (and Soulen) prefer to treat the personal names from a denotative or direct reference viewpoint, while Swain and I prefer a connotative or descriptivist viewpoint.[52] Thus, both Swain and I believe such names as "Father" and "Son" indicate orderly direction in the eternal relations of the persons of the Trinity.

In the third thesis of *God the Trinity*, I asserted the equality of the relations between the Father, the Son, and the Holy Spirit. I chose to use the Eastern language of περιχώρησις (perichoresis) to emphasize that the three persons of the Trinity interact with one another eternally in a dynamic and intimate giving and receiving. Without losing their differentiation, the three persons of the Trinity must be seen as completely indwelling one another such that what the Father is, so

---

[50] R. Kendall Soulen, *The Divine Name(s) and the Holy Trinity: Distinguishing the Voices* (Louisville, KY: Westminster John Knox, 2011).

[51] Grenz, *The Named God and the Question of Being*, 271–80.

[52] See Soulen, *The Divine Name(s) and the Holy Trinity*, 3, 21–23; Grenz, *The Named God and the Question of Being*, 282; Yarnell, *God the Trinity*, 65–67, 121–26; Swain, "Divine Trinity," 88.

is the Son and so is the Holy Spirit.[53] As noted above, Grenz focused on the dynamic activity of love between the three, summarizing his Augustinian appropriation as *via amoris*,[54] and I agree to a significant extent. Elsewhere in his corpus, drawing on his theological training and his fascination with postmodernism, Grenz emphasizes the social, relational, and communal nature of the three persons of the Trinity. On his part, Swain emphasizes "prosopological exegesis," which allows biblical interpreters to perceive the dynamic eternal and economic relations between the Father, the Son, and the Holy Spirit;[55] I agreed here as well. Finally, from an economic perspective, all three of us affirm the inseparable operations of the three divine persons in numerous places.

On the fourth thesis, however, I diverge from Grenz and Swain. As noted above, Grenz demonstrated a preference for the "horizontal" nature of the "noetic model" that he spotted in Victorinus and Augustine. In contrast, both Swain and I lean toward a more "vertical" model. Swain emphasizes that the Trinity's personal names indicate "relations of origin" and that the Father is the "principle or fontal source" of the Son and the Spirit.[56] He also speaks of an "ordered rela-

---

[53] Yarnell, *God the Trinity*, 229.

[54] Grenz, *The Named God and the Question of Being*, 335–40; Yarnell, *God the Trinity*, 46–49.

[55] Swain, "Divine Trinity," 91; Yarnell, *God the Trinity*, 13, 53.

[56] Swain, "Divine Trinity," 88, 99. Both Swain and I note that the eternal ordering of the Trinity is an intra-Reformed dispute championed on the more egalitarian side by John Calvin and especially B. B. Warfield. See also Scott R. Swain, "Inaugural Lecture, Reformed Theological Seminary," November 3, 2015, accessed May 23, 2016, https://www.facebook.com/rtsorlando/posts/10153627935471351. The manuscript for this lecture may be accessed in the April 2018 edition of *Themelios*. See http://themelios.thegospelcoalition .org/article/b-b-warfield-and-the-biblical-doctrine-of-the-trinity, accessed June 20, 2018. For more on this, one may also see Justin Taylor, "What B. B. Warfield Got Wrong in the Doctrine of the Trinity," The Gospel Coalition, February 17, 2016, accessed May 23, 2016, https://blogs.thegospelcoalition.org/justint aylor/2016/02/17/what-b-b-warfield-got-wrong-in-his-doctrine-of-the-trinity/. Cf. Yarnell, *God the Trinity*, 175–76.

tion" between the Father and the Son. Similarly, I emphasized in my book that there is "a proper ordering within the eternal Trinity." The Cappadocian fathers detected a τάξις (*taxis*) between the Father, the Son, and the Holy Spirit, and I concur with their exegetical conclusion. However, like the same Nicene fathers, I also indicated that this ordering "does not entail any loss of equality."[57] On the other hand, it should be noted that Grenz recognized that Augustine requires some "corrective" by the Cappadocians, though he was not forthcoming on the specific outworking of this Cappadocian corrective.

To summarize our discussion of how evangelicals understand God's revelation of himself, the reader should note the substantial agreement between the positions presented here, especially regarding the first three theses of trinitarian ontology: the unitary being of God, the threefold set of ontological relations in God, and the shared equality and indwelling reality of the three persons. While all arrived at these truths in various ways—biblical, historical, and philosophical—the results agree. Yes, Swain and I disagree with Grenz on the ordering of the triune relations. We detect a proper order within God, while Grenz emphasizes a horizontal equality. These theological divergences will result in certain differences in anthropology.

Plausibility of Trinitarian-Anthropological Analogy

To rehearse our method, we affirmed, first, that a theological anthropology must begin with trinitarian theology and not vice versa. Second, we discovered that God may reveal himself to us as he really is, and that he has done so. Any inability to perceive such revelation clearly is not due to a lack in revelation, but to a limitation within humanity, compounded by sinfulness. Third, we found there to be evangelical agreement about three of my four theses regarding the pattern of reality

---

[57] Yarnell, *God the Trinity*, 229–30.

found in God the Trinity. It is in the last thesis, the ordering of the persons in the Trinity, where substantial diversity arises. This brings us to the fourth stage of our theological method: God the Trinity reveals humanity to be created in his image.

Before proceeding to a preliminary affirmation of what the *imago Dei* entails, we must consider a preliminary question: Should we even attempt to define human reality as a reflection of trinitarian reality? For many scholars, especially those with deep roots in the Augustinian tradition, the answer is obviously affirmative. Augustine's illustration of the triune reality was predicated on the image of God located in the mind of man. On the basis of his psychological analogy of God as "memory," "knowledge," and "will," which was closely correlated with his relational analogy of God as "lover," "beloved," and "love," Augustine believed man could ascend to God by moving into the human mind.[58] The inward movement of man into himself is key to the upward movement of man toward God.[59]

Among our three evangelical theologians, Stanley Grenz fully embraced the understanding of God as Trinity from the social perspective of the *imago Dei* well before he ever began to approach the internal structure of divine ontology. Any review of Grenz's works will establish this Augustinian presupposition.[60] For Grenz, the Augustinian approach is axiomatic: one perceives divine reality through human reality. Grenz definitely correlates divine ontology with human ontology.

---

[58] See Augustine, *De Trinitate*, bk. 8, for his doctrine of trinitarian love; bks. 9–15 for his psychological analogy.

[59] Phillip Cary, *Augustine's Invention of the Inner Self: The Legacy of a Christian Platonist* (New York: Oxford University Press, 2000).

[60] This presupposition remained true for Grenz into his final major project, *The Matrix of Christian Theology*. The first volume was titled *The Social God and the Relational Self* and subtitled *A Trinitarian Theology of the Imago Dei*. It was five years later that his final book, on trinitarian ontology, appeared.

Perhaps in reaction to such anthropological optimism, Scott Swain is much more cautious about correlating theology and anthropology. Concluding his summative essay on the biblical and theological basis for the divine Trinity, Swain considers three applications of trinitarian doctrine. He begins with a stark warning: "It would be perverse to construct a doctrine of the Trinity on the basis of a perceived relevance to the needs of creatures rather than from the resources of divine revelation."[61] The choice of the word "perverse" resonates. Despite the strong negative aspect of this warning, Swain does not delimit all movement from the things of God to the things of man. Rather, he places a much-needed stop before the reader to keep him or her from proceeding too quickly. He then goes on to argue that the Trinity can shed light on both theological and practical issues. Swain does not consider anthropology from a trinitarian perspective in his edited systematic volume, but one of his contributors, Kelly Kapic, does.[62]

Swain stands in a long line of orthodox writers when he considers communion with God and God's redemption of humanity as an essential outworking of the doctrine of God the Trinity.[63] It is instructive that the early church fathers, who bequeathed to us the widely received creeds of the church, did not fashion a universally accepted trinitarian anthropology. Instead, they moved from the Trinity into

---

[61] Swain, "Divine Trinity," 102.

[62] Kelly M. Kapic, "Anthropology," in Allen and Swain, *Christian Dogmatics*, 166–67.

[63] Swain, "Divine Trinity," 105. While we note Swain's affirmation of the need to discuss trinitarian redemption of humanity, we have not received his Reformed construal of that movement. Swain argues for the covenant of redemption, not from the perspective of biblical exegesis, but as a "gloss of biblical teaching." The lack of exegesis in the second of Swain's two trinitarian essays, especially in comparison with his first essay, is significant. Swain, "Covenant of Redemption," in Allen and Swain, *Christian Dogmatics*, 107–25, especially 109. See Yarnell, *God the Trinity*, 230.

the doctrines of the atonement and of the salvation of humanity. A careful reading of the three major trinitarian traditions from the early church—the Apostles' Creed, the Nicene Creed, and the Athanasian Creed[64]—should demonstrate this severely restricted movement. Swain rightly issues a stark warning against proceeding too quickly between anthropology and theology. And Swain's stop sign should stay with us, encouraging us to take care and refrain from reading our contemporary concerns and ideas back into the biblical text, even as we beg God to enlighten our minds regarding the contemporary and very practical implications of his Word.

We do believe, however, that when performed with utmost caution a movement from trinitarian theology into theological anthropology benefits theological discourse. In his contribution to *A Manifesto for Theological Interpretation*, Heath A. Thomas argues that reading Scripture ought to impact the totality of human life. "God provides Scripture to the church for its transformation into the image of Christ, by the power of the Spirit."[65] Moreover, such theological reading of the Bible "ought to press toward the formation of the whole person and the totality of the church: cognitive, emotional, social, spatial, and psychological."[66] With Swain's warning against moving too quickly into anthropology and Thomas's affirmation of the reading of Scripture for the purpose of transforming humanity, we now turn to a short presentation of the structure of humanity from a trinitarian perspective.

---

[64] We have provided new translations of the Symbolum Apostolicum, Symbolum Nicaeno-Constantinopolinatum, and the Symbolum Quicunque in an appendix. See Yarnell, *God the Trinity*, 240–43.

[65] Heath A. Thomas, "The Telos (Goal) of Theological Interpretation," in *A Manifesto for Theological Interpretation*, ed. Craig G. Bartholomew and Heath A. Thomas (Grand Rapids: Baker Academic, 2016), 205.

[66] Thomas, 205.

God the Trinity Reveals Humanity
to Be Created in His Image

From Irenaeus to John Calvin, it was affirmed that God's creation of humanity in his image was a trinitarian activity.[67] But the modern critics sundered these canonical connections. Upon reviewing the literature, Karl Barth concluded that the moderns were guilty of hubris, of "arrogant rejection."[68] While the Trinity is not explicitly revealed in Genesis 1–3, there are several indications that any Christian reading of this seminal text requires a trinitarian understanding of God. The three persons of the Trinity appear obliquely either in their person or their work in Gen 1:1–3, but they each appear clearly in other biblical texts as working inseparably in the divine act of creation.[69] In turning to the key verses of 1:26–27, many have suggested that the presence of plurality and singularity is expressed in these verses, both within the creating God and within his reflection, the creature man.

In the twentieth century, Dietrich Bonhoeffer, Karl Barth, and Emil Brunner helped establish the now nearly universal belief that God as Trinity creates humanity in his image. Bonhoeffer was the innovative scholar in this development, but Barth and Brunner popularized his findings.[70] In *Creation and Fall*, Bonhoeffer cited the older Lutheran

---

[67] Irenaeus, *Against Heresies*, 4.20.1, in *The Apostolic Fathers, Justin Martyr, Irenaeus*, ed. Alexander Roberts and James Donaldson, Ante-Nicene Fathers, vol. 1 (reprint, Peabody, MA: Hendrickson, 1994), 487; John Calvin, *Commentaries on the First Book of Moses Called Genesis*, trans. John King, vol. 1 (reprint, Grand Rapids: Baker, 1996), 91–93.

[68] Karl Barth, *Church Dogmatics* 3.1, *The Doctrine of Creation*, ed. G. W. Bromiley and T. F. Torrance, trans. J. W. Edwards, O. Bussey, and H. Knight (Edinburgh: T&T Clark, 1958), 191–95. Cf. Grenz, *The Social God and the Relational Self*, 285–87.

[69] Yarnell, *God the Trinity*, 190–91.

[70] Barth credits Bonhoeffer, and Brunner credits Barth. Barth, *Church Dogmatics* 3.1, 194–95; Emil Brunner, *The Christian Doctrine of Creation and Redemption*, Christian Dogmatics, vol. 2, trans. Olive Wyon (Philadelphia: Westminster Press, 1952), 63–65.

dogmatic theologians, who "spoke of the indwelling of the Trinity in Adam," but Bonhoeffer developed this in a relational direction: "The creature is free in that one creature exists in relation to another creature, in that one human being is free for another human being. And God created them man and woman. The human being is not alone. Human beings exist in duality, and it is in this *dependence on the other that their creatureliness consists.*"[71]

For Bonhoeffer, because God in his plurality is free Creator beholding free Creator, his image is freedom for the creature as the "other." Such freedom for the human being means that he may worship God fully with praise.[72] Bonhoeffer rejects the traditional substantive view of the *imago Dei* with its dependence on the *analogia entis* (analogy of being), preferring instead to see the likeness between God and humanity as an *analogia relationis* (analogy of relation).[73] As relational beings made in the image of the relational God, human beings exist "over-against-one-another, with-one-another, and in-dependence-upon-one-another."[74] Bonhoeffer also reminds the reader there are limits to the analogy between God and man. The image of God is like God in that it "derives its likeness only from the prototype, so that it always points us only to the prototype itself and is 'like' it only in pointing to it in this way."[75]

Bonhoeffer also raises the matter of the divine image as relational in his review of the so-called "second creation story," which he believes is not unlike the first creation account. Rather, the two creation stories say or represent "the same thing from two different sides."[76] On

---

[71] Italics his. Dietrich Bonhoeffer, *Creation and Fall: A Theological Exposition of Genesis 1–3*, ed. John W. de Gruchy, trans. Douglas Stephen Bax, Dietrich Bonhoeffer Works, vol. 3 (Minneapolis: Fortress, 1997), 64.

[72] Bonhoeffer, 61.

[73] Bonhoeffer, 65.

[74] Bonhoeffer, 64.

[75] Bonhoeffer, 65.

[76] Bonhoeffer, 71.

this basis, Bonhoeffer used Gen 2:18–25 to work out more fully the relational nature of the divine image as male and female revealed in Gen 1:26–27.

As a sovereign act, God made the woman from man so that man would not be alone. She is derived from him, and she is made for him as a divine gift. The joyous unity and plurality of humanity is a divine mystery. Bonhoeffer captures this mystery with these words: "They have from their origin been one, and only in becoming one do they return to their origin."[77] Eve, in being for the other, Adam, is "a helper who is a partner," for she embodies Adam's limit and is the object of Adam's love. "Indeed love for the woman was now to be the human being's very life (in the deepest sense of the word)."[78] As both a real "limit for me" and "piece of me," Adam and Eve find themselves bonded freely in love. In their embodied sexuality is expressed "the two complementary sides of the matter: that of being an individual and that of being one with the other."[79] The freedom of love found in the garden relationship between Adam and Eve shows that marriage with its sexuality is a divine gift. The sexuality of marriage is also the basis of all human community, including the church.[80] The fall, alas, has turned the gift of sexuality into selfishness and shame.[81]

We do not find any reason to doubt the general claim that relations within God are the basis for the male-female relation and thence all relations within humanity. With the premodern theologians and with many theologians since Bonhoeffer's formulation, we find the *imago Dei* reflects God in his singular and relational reality. Proceeding from anthropology to ethics, or reality to relevance, we also believe

---

[77] Bonhoeffer, 97.

[78] Bonhoeffer, 98–99.

[79] Bonhoeffer, 99–100.

[80] Bonhoeffer, 100. Grenz will develop this thought in particular, as he moves from emphasizing the social and the relational to focusing on community. Grenz, *The Social God and the Relational Self*, 303.

[81] Bonhoeffer, *Creation and Fall*, 101.

this is fruitful for a recovery of concern for the dignity of the "other." As a result of sin, human societies have become fractured by war and oppression within nations, races, and religions, and even within families. These general findings are relatively uncontroversial among evangelical Christians. On the one hand, one prominent gender complementarian, Bruce A. Ware, believes the relevance of the trinitarian reflection includes hope for a beautiful "harmony" and "love" in human relationships.[82] On the other hand, a prominent gender egalitarian, Millard J. Erickson, believes the trinitarian reflection means every human being has "value" and is "important."[83]

However, the exposition becomes controversial, especially among contemporary evangelicals, when construing how the relational nature of humanity is instantiated within the communion of male and female.[84] Perceiving the presence of gender relation in the *imago Dei* from Genesis 1 does not mean the structure of that relation is evident from the same text.[85] In order to move from the reality of the gender relations as reflective of God as Trinity into the structure of these gender relations requires turning to other biblical texts. There are indications of such a structure, but they are not evident to every biblical

---

[82] Ware emphasizes "harmony." Bruce A. Ware, *Father, Son, & Holy Spirit: Relationships, Roles, & Relevance* (Wheaton, IL: Crossway, 2005), 133–38

[83] Millard J. Erickson, *Making Sense of the Trinity: Three Crucial Questions* (Grand Rapids: Baker, 2000), 96–99.

[84] A helpful volume drawing together many authors from all sides of this controversy is Dennis W. Jowers and H. Wayne House, eds., *The New Evangelical Subordinationism? Perspectives on the Equality of God the Father and God the Son* (Eugene, OR: Pickwick, 2012).

[85] In Gen 2:18–25, the interpretation of "helper" and the derivation of Eve from Adam are, however, potentially significant. Bonhoeffer seems to flatten the relation between Adam and Eve in his treatment, even as he emphasizes the distinctions and dependence between the two sexes. "The grace of the other person's being our helper who is a partner because *he or she* helps us to bear our limit, that is, helps us to live before God—and we can live before God only in community with our helper." Italics mine. Bonhoeffer, *Creation and Fall*, 99.

exegete, as Hongyi Yang's recent perceptive review of the lacunae in the trinitarian gender debate demonstrates.[86]

In her balanced and judicious critique of treatments of Scripture and history by both egalitarian scholars and complementarian scholars, Yang believes there is textual evidence for an orderly correlation between the Trinity's internal reality and humanity's internal reality. If the Genesis text does demonstrate an orderly structure, then our method requires a movement toward a complementarian outlook. Yang believes that 1 Cor 11:3 presents the divine relation between Christ and God as necessarily ordered and analogous for the human relation between a man and woman: "But I want you to know that Christ is the head [κεφαλή] of every man, and the man is the head [κεφαλή] of a woman, and God [θεός] is the head [κεφαλή] of Christ."

The critical issues in this text for our subject include the meaning of κεφαλή, the identity of θεός, and the placement of the exclusively divine relation in either the economic or the immanent Trinity. First, Yang believes κεφαλή most likely means "head." But even if the interpreter were to opt for the major alternative of "source," this "cannot exclude" the meaning of "hierarchical order."[87] Second, Yang notes that by θεός the New Testament typically refers to the Father, and that interpreters throughout Christian history have overwhelmingly opted for understanding θεός here as the Father.[88] Third, with regard to whether the headship of the Father is immanent or economic, Yang argues that placing the Father's headship over the Son only in time would mean that Christ's headship over man would also come to an end, which she finds ludicrous and a contradiction of 1 Cor 15:28.[89] Kyle Claunch, a

---

[86] Hongyi Yang, "A Development Not a Departure: The Lacunae in the Debate of the Doctrine of the Trinity and Gender Roles" (PhD diss., Southwestern Baptist Theological Seminary, 2016).

[87] Yang, 61.

[88] Yang, 56–58.

[89] Yang, 63–65.

complementarian, argues, alternatively, that 1 Cor 11:3 applies to the economic Trinity directly but to the immanent Trinity indirectly.[90]

Eschatological Caution

Our theological method has affirmed the following: First, we must proceed from theology toward anthropology, and we must move with great caution in the reverse direction. Second, God's revelation of his reality is trustworthy. Third, God has revealed himself to be constituted in unity, with a threefold set of personal relations, which are characterized by both perichoretic equality and certain order. Fourth, we discovered that humanity was created in the divine image as located in the relation of the first man and his wife. Much of this is agreed upon within the contemporary literature, except for the internal and eternal ordering of the divine persons that many have perceived but others have denied. Now, we must draw these conclusions together with a few words of caution.

We are primarily concerned with the image of God. This is not the place to define or demonstrate a complete doctrine of the *imago Dei*,[91] but we wish to erect four warning signs from that fuller doctrine. First, while we affirm Bonhoeffer's relational approach, we also find value in the substantive and functional approaches. Second, Scripture implies that the image has been harmed in the fall, although it remains

---

[90] If Claunch rather than Yang is correct here, then the movement toward complementarianism from the Trinity depends on some reception of Rahner's Rule. Kyle Claunch, "God Is the Head of Christ: Does 1 Corinthians 11:3 Ground Gender Complementarity in the Immanent Trinity?" in *One God in Three Persons: Unity of Essence, Distinction of Persons, Implications for Life*, ed. Bruce A. Ware and John Stark (Wheaton, IL: Crossway, 2015), 78–87.

[91] My first systematic volume, *The Formation of Christian Doctrine*, concerned theological method. The second, *God the Trinity*, concerned God in his triune being and acts. In my third systematic volume, provisionally titled, *The Image of the Trinity*, I hope to focus on the Trinity's impact on humanity.

present and is deemed valuable to God. Third, while humanity was created *in* the divine image, Jesus Christ himself *is* the divine image. This distinction drives us toward Christology for a proper anthropology. Fourth, the divine image in redeemed humanity is currently being transformed into the fullness of that image. This fourth warning, an eschatological caution, jams open the gate of contemporary dogmatic construction. According to Scripture, the definitions provided therein manifestly do not tell us everything about what humanity will become (but it does tell us much). While numerous texts could be cited, three come immediately to mind. First, in 1 Cor 15:49, we are told the created image is not the final image: "as we have borne the image of the man made of dust, we will also bear the image of the heavenly man" (HCSB). Drawing on an Adam-Christ typology, Paul asserted that the created *imago Dei*, even in its pristine state, is not the end of the *imago Dei*. There is an undeniable dynamism in the divine image of humanity. The Lord himself taught that while human beings are constituted in the holy covenant of marriage, marriage does not complete humanity (Mark 12:25 and parallels).

A second biblical text considers the triune God's ongoing activity of transforming humanity: "We all, with unveiled faces, are looking as in a mirror at the glory of the Lord and are being transformed into the same image from glory to glory; this is from the Lord who is the Spirit" (2 Cor 3:18 CSB). Paul is using the experience of Moses with Yahweh in Exodus 34 to show that God is currently changing Christians into the image of the mirror, which is Christ (2 Cor 4:6). This transformation of humanity into the divine image is occurring now, since the verb for transformation is in the present tense. But it is not yet complete. It moves "from glory to glory," evoking not only Moses in the wilderness but also the glory expected in the second coming (e.g., Col 1:24; 3:7). To round off the trinitarian transformation of man, Paul affirms that the Father's conformation of us to Jesus Christ is the continuing work of the Holy Spirit.

A third text that places a roadblock before those who wish to close out the definition of trinitarian anthropology is 1 John 3:2: "Dear friends, we are God's children now, and what we will be has not yet been revealed. We know that when he appears, we will be like him because we will see him as he is" (CSB). Simply put, the fullness of human anthropology is currently unavailable to us: "what we will be has not yet been revealed." As the late Ian Howard Marshall noted, "The contrast is between the known and the unknown." This is a cause for hope rather than despair: "[O]ur knowledge of our present state enables us to say that our future state will be something even more wonderful."[92] We know God is currently transforming us into something like Christ, particularly his righteousness that is our righteousness (1 John 2:29). We also know that a fuller revelation of what we will become awaits Christ's second coming (παρουσία; 1 John 2:28). He has not yet come again, so we cannot see him. But when we see him, we will be found in his likeness, "because we will see him as he is" (1 John 3:2 CSB). The clouds concealing fuller knowledge of divine and human ontology—whether the source of blindness is in our created limits, our fallen nature, or a lack of full revelation—will be dispersed by the eminent and immediate presence of the perfect image of God, Jesus Christ. Only then will our theological anthropology be fully disclosed.

Until that time, we must be careful with the doctrinal claims we make about the relationship between the internal reality of God as Trinity and the external relations of humanity in family, church, and society. While the revelation of God teaches an order within the Trinity, and while that order is reflected in human marriage, it would be hasty to assume the issue has been entirely closed. The strain of evangelical brothers and sisters holding to opposing views of complementarianism and egalitarianism brings discomfort, but all sides must carefully

---

[92] I. Howard Marshall, *The Epistles of John*, The New International Commentary on the New Testament (Grand Rapids: Eerdmans, 1978), 171.

evaluate the withdrawal of fellowship, the hurling of inflammatory and unnecessary accusations of trinitarian heresy, and the accusations of apostasy. There remain legitimate methodological questions regarding the denotative or connotative nature of names, the truthful extent of Rahner's axiom, and a myriad of similar exegetical judgments. These questions are significant enough to demand caution on my part before requiring my own construal of trinitarian gender complementarianism as *sine qua non* for theological anthropology, although I am personally convinced this is the proper way forward.

CHAPTER 3

On Trinitarian Theological Method

BY MATTHEW Y. EMERSON AND LUKE STAMPS

Introduction

What makes a doctrine biblical?[1] This is the fundamental question of
theological method. In some sense, all Christian theologians desire
to be biblical in their doctrinal formulations. This is true of Roman
Catholic, Eastern Orthodox, and Protestant theologians alike. But the
sense that our doctrines should be grounded in Scripture is perhaps
especially acute among evangelical Protestants, given our commitment
to the Reformation principles of *sola scriptura* (Scripture alone) and
semper reformanda secundum verbum Dei (always reforming according to

---

[1] Kevin Vanhoozer speaks of his own "holy grail" quest for an answer to the
question: "What does it mean to be biblical?" See Kevin J. Vanhoozer, "From
Canon to Concept: 'Same' and 'Other' in the Relation between Biblical and
Systematic Theology," *Scottish Bulletin of Evangelical Theology* 12, no. 2 (Autumn
1994): 96–124.

the Word of God). Thus, in a Protestant theological method, all eccle-
siastical institutions and councils must be subjected to the ultimate
authority of Holy Scripture.

But does the evangelical commitment to Scripture's sole, final
authority mean that classical theological formulations carry no authority in the formation of biblical doctrines? Perhaps surprisingly to some
(and less surprisingly to others), certain evangelical theologians have
questioned classical—even creedal—doctrines by appeal to *sola scriptura*. For example, Wayne Grudem has called for the removal of the
descensus clause from the Apostles' Creed[2] and at one time raised
doubts about eternal generation, the linchpin of pro-Nicene trinitarianism.[3] Similarly, evangelical philosophers J. P. Moreland, William
Lane Craig, and Garrett DeWeese have questioned the traditional doctrine of Christ's two wills.[4] Moreland and Craig have even suggested a
rehabilitation of a version of Apollinaris's Christology (although with
some modifications).[5] In these and other scenarios like them, some

---

[2] Wayne Grudem, "He Did Not Descend into Hell: A Plea for Following
Scripture instead of the Apostles' Creed," *JETS* 34, no. 1 (March 1991): 103–13.
Grudem's subtitle expresses succinctly this alleged dichotomy between Scripture
and the ecumenical creeds.

[3] See Wayne Grudem, *Systematic Theology: An Introduction to Biblical Doctrine*
(Grand Rapids: Zondervan, 1994, 2000), appendix 6. It should be noted that at
a recent panel discussion in conjunction with the 2016 Annual Meeting of the
Evangelical Theological Society, Grudem says that he now affirms the eternal
relations of origin.

[4] J. P. Moreland and William Lane Craig, *Philosophical Foundations for a
Christian Worldview* (Downers Grove, IL: IVP Academic, 2003), 611. Garret
DeWeese, "One Person, Two Natures: Two Metaphysical Models of the
Incarnation," in *Jesus in Trinitarian Perspective: An Introductory Christology*, ed. by
Fred Sanders and Klaus Issler (Nashville, TN: B&H Academic, 2007), 114–53.

[5] Moreland and Craig, *Philosophical Foundations*, 609. To be clear, Moreland
and Craig admit that Apollinaris's view was "radically defective as it stood." But
they suggest a revision to his view (arguing that the Logos possessed the properties of human personhood latently, "lacking only corporeality") that they prefer
to the traditional two-wills Christology.

evangelical theologians feel warranted in rejecting consensus doctrinal positions if they, as individual theologians and philosophers, remain unconvinced by their biblical support.

From our vantage point, these departures from classical Christian doctrine are largely a function of theological method. More specifically, we posit that, in many of these departures, some version of biblicism is the method of choice. Though we finally diverge from the biblicist approach, we do not intend to use the term pejoratively but, rather, descriptively: a biblicist is one who seeks to interpret the biblical text, as far as is possible, without any outside influence, particularly any undue creedal or confessional influence. In this approach, appeal to Scripture seeks for straightforward readings and often involves some version of proof texting: the compilation of biblical texts that purportedly demand a given theological conclusion. Biblicism is critical of readings that make too frequent or too strong an appeal to traditional commitments, especially when those commitments seem to run counter to the "plain" meaning of specific biblical texts. Biblicists are not necessarily dismissive of traditional readings, but they believe theologizing should concern itself first and foremost with the language of Scripture and only secondarily with extra-biblical theological formulations.[6]

This essay contends there is a way to be thoroughly *biblical* without succumbing to the drawbacks of *biblicism*, and one of the primary test cases for this methodological distinction is the doctrine of the Trinity. Therefore, we wish to articulate a canonical, confessional, and dogmatically informed evangelical theological method. We wish to retain the biblicist commitment to *sola scriptura* while at the same time operating with what might be called a "thick biblicism," in which what counts as biblical encompasses something much more than simply

---

[6] For a nuanced defense of biblicism, see John M. Frame, "In Defense of Something Close to Biblicism: Reflections on *Sola Scriptura* and History in Theological Method," *WTJ* 59, no. 2 (Fall 1997): 269–91.

collating "plain" readings of biblical texts. To put it simply, a canonical, confessional, and dogmatic theological method seeks to articulate Christian doctrine by understanding Scripture as a canonical whole, read in light of the Church's consensual tradition,[7] and with the aid of dogmatic reasoning. The method articulated below also situates the task of theology primarily in an ecclesial context in which the Spirit's illuminating guidance is a nonnegotiable factor.

The essay will proceed in two steps. First, we will articulate and defend more fully the method outlined above; second, we will sketch in broad strokes the kind of trinitarian doctrine that this method yields.

On Theological Method

In our teaching and writing ministries, we are constantly thinking through what it means to interpret Scripture faithfully—not only to interpret individual biblical texts but also to do so in light of the larger canon of Scripture and in light of the faith that was "once for all delivered to the saints" (Jude 3).[8] Grounded in the thinking of St. Augustine and St. Anselm, we wish to follow a method of *fides quaerens intellectum*—faith seeking understanding.[9] This tradition places an epistemic priority on personal trust in God and his revelation, from which we then press on to a deeper understanding of what has been revealed. We believe that this method best captures what we see both in the

---

[7] This is the language of Thomas Oden, who views the great tradition as grounded in ecumenical lay consensus. See Thomas C. Oden, *Classic Christianity: A Systematic Theology* (New York: Harper Collins, 1987–92).

[8] Unless otherwise noted, all Scripture citations in this chapter are from the English Standard Version (ESV).

[9] For an introduction to *fides quaerens intellectum* from historical and theological vantage points, see Scott Swain, *Trinity, Revelation, and Reading: A Theological Introduction to the Bible and Its Interpretation*, T&T Clark Theology (London: T&T Clark, 2011), 1–11; and Kevin J. Vanhoozer, *The Drama of Doctrine: A Canonical Linguistic Approach to Christian Theology* (Louisville, KY: Westminster John Knox, 2005), especially 16–24, 151–242.

New Testament, where the apostles sought to understand Jesus in light of the Law and the Prophets, and also in the post-apostolic church, which sought to interpret the Christ-event in light of the divine *oikonomia* revealed in Scripture.[10] Neither the New Testament authors nor the early church theologians believed they were developing doctrines apart from what had already been passed down to them. We will return to the place of tradition in due course, but for now our point is simply this: we cannot approach theological method under the guise of some supposed neutrality without acknowledging our precommitments.[11] We approach Scripture with eyes of faith, eyes renewed by God the Spirit through the work of God the Son to the glory of God the Father.[12]

Spirit-Led and Ecclesially Located

This brings us to the first aspect of our theological method, its pneumatological element. An evangelical theological method recognizes the interpreter's reliance on the Holy Spirit for understanding and applying the Word of God. This means that if we are to read and understand Scripture in accordance with God's purposes for it—namely, our transformation into Christ's image (2 Cor 3:17–18)—then we must read in a way that is guided by the Spirit. Because biblical interpretation and

---

[10] See the helpful work of John J. O'Keefe and R. R. Reno, *Sanctified Vision: An Introduction to Early Christian Interpretation of the Bible* (Baltimore: Johns Hopkins University Press, 2005).

[11] On precommitments and interpretation, see, for example, Jeannine K. Brown, *Scripture as Communication: Introducing Biblical Hermeneutics* (Grand Rapids: Baker Academic, 2007), 88–90. See also James K. A. Smith, *The Fall of Interpretation: Philosophical Foundations for a Creational Hermeneutic*, 2nd ed. (Grand Rapids: Baker Academic, 2012) for an attempt to understand interpretive variance from the perspective of human creatureliness.

[12] See J. Todd Billings, *The Word of God for the People of God: An Entryway to the Theological Interpretation of Scripture* (Grand Rapids: Eerdmans, 2010), 1–30; and John Webster, *Holy Scripture: A Dogmatic Sketch*, Current Issues in Theology (Cambridge: Cambridge University Press, 2003), 86.

theological reflection are ultimately intended to bring us into communion with the triune God and transform us into Christ's image, these endeavors must be grounded in reliance on God's Spirit if they are to be performed faithfully.[13] We are confident that other Christian theologians, whose methodologies may differ from ours in certain respects, are no less committed to this same reliance on the Spirit's help. So we do not include this point by way of contrast with any particular methodology, but simply to lay the right foundation from the outset. Another foundational claim that we suspect is shared by all Christian theologians, in some sense or other, is that doctrinal reflection is to be situated primarily in the context of the church. This point, too, is pneumatological, since it is the Spirit of God who gives birth to the church's faith and who guides the church through his inspired Word. We read Scripture in community with one another as the body of Christ, as an exercise in humility and accountability (e.g., Phil 2:1–4).[14] The primary place of biblical and theological formation is the local church, but ultimately the community in which we read Holy Scripture stretches throughout time and space, bringing in its train all the saints of all the ages (*communio sanctorum*).

Exegetically Grounded

A second aspect of our proposed theological method here is its exegetical grounding. We do not commend any weak, surface-level interaction with the biblical text, but instead we propose a rigorous engagement with individual passages of Scripture in our doctrinal formulations.[15] Again, this is common ground for many theological methods and particularly for those who would identify in some way as "biblicist." Indeed, many times doctrines are based on explicit

---

[13] See, for example, Vanhoozer, *Drama of Doctrine*, 65.

[14] On reading in community, see John Webster, *Word and Church*, Essays in Church Dogmatics (London: T&T Clark, 2001), 3–47.

[15] See Billings, *Word of God*, 31–70.

exegetical arguments pertaining to one or perhaps a very few passages in Scripture; one example is the doctrine of the resurrection of the body. While the hope of bodily resurrection is found in a number of places, 1 Corinthians 15 is one of very few passages that inform us about the particulars of this doctrine. Exegesis of this text can get us a long way toward formulating a doctrine of the bodily resurrection.

Canonically Patterned

In some cases, exegesis of one or a few passages is not enough, nor is it even possible for some doctrines to be formulated in this way. For instance, while the Scriptures express the *reality* of the Trinity (that God is one and that the Father, Son, and Holy Spirit are distinct and yet each is to be identified and worshiped as God), they do not give us, in any conceptually precise sense, the *doctrine* of the Trinity. In other words, we cannot simply proof text the linchpin doctrines of Nicene trinitarianism, such as eternal generation or the *homoousion*. Instead, we must consider the shape of the canon and the various horizons of biblical interpretation.[16] One way this occurs is through the patterns of biblical language, which give us insight into certain doctrinal truths. David Yeago, in "The New Testament and the Nicene Dogma,"[17] argues that dogmatics is the measured use of conceptual terms to make correct judgments about these biblical patterns. Yeago's point is that often particular doctrines are grounded not in a few select biblical verses, but in broader patterns of biblical language. So, for instance, the doctrine of eternal generation does not stand or fall on one or two passages (say, Prov 8:22–31 or John 5:26), but is instead grounded in the pattern

---

[16] On the horizons of biblical interpretation (textual, epochal, and canonical), see Richard Lints, *The Fabric of Theology: A Prolegomenon to Evangelical Theology* (Grand Rapids: Eerdmans, 1993), 293–310.

[17] David Yeago, "The New Testament and Nicene Dogma," in *The Theological Interpretation of Scripture: Classic and Contemporary Readings*, ed. Stephen E. Fowl (Oxford: Blackwell, 1997), 87–100.

we see expressed in Father-Son language throughout Scripture.[18] The broad patterns of Scripture need to be considered. These patterns are not limited to one text, nor are they always particularly reliant on fastidious exegesis of particular texts.[19] Rather, to see Father-Son language referring to the first and second persons of God throughout the Bible is to recognize that Scripture identifies Father and Son as sharing a common essence via the analogy of Father-Son (more on this below). As Yeago argues, while some may formulate their doctrine of the Trinity using different conceptual language from Scripture (e.g., *homoousios*), the same theological judgments about the identity of Jesus Christ with relation to the Father should still be rendered.

Scripture and its interpretation are canonically patterned in other ways as well. The Bible is an intertextual tapestry,[20] so if we are to exegete a passage properly, we must locate it within its immediate, redemptive-historical, and canonical contexts. We must also interpret Scripture narratively.[21] In sum, being "biblical" does mean exegeting particu-

---

[18] For a classic treatment of Proverbs 8, see Gregory of Nyssa, *Against Eunomius* 1.1.34, *NPNF* 5. On the treatment of Proverbs 8 in Athanasius, see Lewis Ayres, *Nicaea and Its Legacy: An Approach to Fourth-Century Trinitarian Theology* (Oxford: Oxford University Press, 2004), 113–14. On the Father-Son language in Paul as inherently relational, see Wesley Hill, *Paul and the Trinity: Persons, Relations, and the Pauline Letters* (Grand Rapids, MI: Eerdmans, 2015).

[19] For example, much ink has been spilt in recent years on the precise etymology of *monogenes* in John's Gospel. Does it derive from *gennao* (to beget) or from *genos* (kind)? While we think a strong case can be made for the former, the doctrine of eternal generation does not stand or fall based on that narrow semantic debate.

[20] On this tapestry-like theological method, see Matthew Y. Emerson, *Christ and the New Creation: A Canonical Approach to the Theology of the New Testament* (Eugene, OR: Wipf & Stock, 2013), 6–13. For a classic definition of intertextuality in Scripture, see Richard B. Hays, *Echoes of Scripture in the Letters of Paul* (New Haven, CT: Yale University Press, 1989), 14–21.

[21] This narrative pattern of Scripture is commonly known as the "economy" of Scripture. On the grand narrative of Scripture and its relation to dogmatic reflection, see, for example, Lints, *The Fabric of Theology*, 259–89.

lar passages, but it also means doing so in light of the Christocentric narrative of Scripture and with a view to broader patterns of biblical language that cannot necessarily be pinned down to a particular text.

Creedally Ruled

A word on terminology as we begin this section: when we speak of a creedally ruled method, we do not mean "ruled" in the sense of "dominate" or "have power over." Rather, we use "ruled" here as a reference to the *regula fidei*, the rule of faith. Defining the rule of faith precisely is a notoriously difficult task; but there are a few elements of which we can be fairly certain.[22] The chief conviction is that the Bible is a narrative—from creation and fall to redemption and restoration— a narrative that centers on the person and work of Jesus Christ, the God-man. Importantly, the rule and these aspects of it are biblically derived, from Luke 24:44, John 5:46, and other such passages.

A second way that biblical interpretation is "ruled" is via creeds and confessions, the role of which it is to accurately reflect the biblical narrative and its teaching.[23] As Protestants, we recognize that creeds and confessions are always subject to revision, given compelling biblical evidence of that necessity.[24] Nevertheless, the three ecumenical

---

[22] For an introduction to the "rule," see Paul Blowers, "The *Regula Fidei* and the Narrative Character of Early Christian Faith," *Pro Ecclesia* 6 no. 2 (1998): 199–228. For its scriptural warrant and role in dogmatic reflection, see Vanhoozer, *The Drama of Doctrine*, 203–11.

[23] On this articulation of creedal authority and its relation to the biblical narrative, see, for instance, Alister E. McGrath, *The Genesis of Doctrine: A Study in the Foundation of Doctrinal Criticism* (Grand Rapids, MI: Eerdmans, 1997), especially 52–65.

[24] The judgment of Oliver Crisp is apt: "It seems to me that someone dissenting from the findings of an ecumenical council of the Church should have a very good reason—indeed, a very good *theological* reason—for doing so." Oliver Crisp, *Divinity and Humanity* (New York: Cambridge University Press, 2007), 35; emphasis original.

creeds (Nicene-Constantinopolitan, Athanasian, and Apostles') and at least the first four ecumenical councils have been accepted as derivatively authoritative by most Protestants, including most evangelicals, throughout our history.[25]

Dogmatically Guided

Finally, dogmatic concerns guide us in answering the question, what is biblical? By "dogmatic" we mean questions of a systematic nature— questions that deal with the logical, theological, and ethical implications of biblical texts and how those implications impinge on the broader fabric of Christian doctrine. Adjusting one area of doctrine ultimately impinges on all the others.

Theological decision making is also dogmatic in the sense that it must give careful attention to the nature of our talk about God. In one sense, we can speak positively about who God is on the basis of his revelation to us, but in another sense, we can only speak about God's essence by saying what he is not (*via negativa*). We are finite creatures, and he is the Creator, so we can know him only in a creaturely way. God's knowledge of himself is archetypal, while our knowledge of him is always ectypal, an imprint and shadow of God's self-knowledge.[26] As we talk about God, then, we must remember that there are some things of which we cannot speak in any positive sense. Even in Scripture, God uses analogical language accommodated to our finitude. As creatures, we cannot describe the essence of God exactly as God knows himself (univocal language). But because he has revealed himself to us, we are

---

[25] For instance, one of the earliest Baptist confessions of faith, the Orthodox Creed of the General Baptists (1678), states in Article 38 that they affirm the three ecumenical Creeds. William L. Lumpkin, eds., *Baptist Confessions of Faith*, ed. Bill J. Leonard, 2nd rev. ed. (Valley Forge, PA: Judson, 1959; repr., 2011), 337–38.

[26] On the archetypal/ectypal distinction, see Herman Bavinck, *Reformed Dogmatics: Holy Spirit, Church, and New Creation*, ed. John Bolt, trans. John Vriend, 4 vols. (Grand Rapids, MI: Baker Academic, 2003), 1:212.

not left in a situation where our language always misses the mark in describing him (equivocal language). Rather, our God-talk is always analogous; creaturely words are analogical pointers to the reality of God in himself.[27]

Concluding Reflections on Method

We see from the method briefly articulated above that determining what is biblical involves not only exegeting particular passages, but also doing so in light of canonical, narrative, and intertextual patterns, the rule of faith, the derivative authority of the creeds, and dogmatic considerations—all in reliance on the Holy Spirit and in the context of the Church. In sum: the method is illumined by the Spirit, rooted in biblical exegesis, governed by patterns of biblical language, shaped by the biblical economy, guided by the biblically derived rule of faith, guarded by biblically derived tradition, refined by systematic and philosophical reflection, and located within the communion of the saints (pp. 12, 105, 141).[28]

On the Trinity

The question remains then: what sort of doctrine of God does this method yield? More specifically: what kind of trinitarianism results from utilizing this biblically grounded, creedally ruled, and dogmatically guided methodology? Articulating a complete doctrine of the Trinity is well beyond the scope of this essay, but in what follows we wish to sketch the main contours of the classical doctrine of the Trinity and its biblical and theological rationale, as we understand them.

---

[27] See Gregory Nazianzen, *First Theological Oration*, 8; also Nazianzen, *Second Theological Oration*, 3, *NPNF* 7.

[28] A version of this paragraph originally appeared on our blog, *Biblical Reasoning*, https://secundumscripturas.com/.

Along the way, we will also have occasion to highlight some of the flash points of controversy that remain between this classical doctrine of the Trinity and some contemporary evangelical proposals.

The biblical basis for a broad trinitarianism is well known and oft rehearsed. On the one hand, the Scriptures consistently affirm that there is (and can only be) one God, who alone is the self-sufficient, eternal, and almighty Creator and sustainer of all that exists. This monotheistic commitment is true of the New Testament (1 Cor 8:6; 1 Tim 2:5) no less than the Old (Deut 6:4).[29] On the other hand, as redemptive history reaches its climax in the New Testament, we learn that the earliest Christians identified three distinct figures—Father, Son, and Holy Spirit—as God without in any way attenuating their commitment to monotheism.[30] The Old Testament had left open the possibility of some kind of plurality in the Godhead—think, for example, of the personified Wisdom who accompanies the divine Creator in Proverbs 8, or of the ways in which the Davidic King is spoken of in divine terms (Ps(s) 45:6; 110:1; Isa 9:6)—but only in the new covenant missions of the Son and Spirit is this plurality made explicit. The Father's deity is assumed throughout the New Testament. The Son's deity is affirmed both explicitly and implicitly, as he assumes the names, attributes, actions, and prerogatives of God himself.[31] Similarly, the Holy Spirit is identified as God and yet as a figure distinct from the Father and Son.[32] And the triadic passages we find in

---

[29] Katherine Sonderegger has rightly reminded us of the canonical and hermeneutical priority of the unity of God. Katherine Sonderegger, *Systematic Theology*, vol. 1, *The Doctrine of God* (Minneapolis, MN: Fortress, 2015).

[30] We are borrowing the language of "identity" from Richard Bauckham's presentation of New Testament Christology. See Richard Bauckham, *Jesus and the God of Israel: God Crucified and Other Studies on the New Testament's Christology of Divine Identity* (Grand Rapids, MI: Eerdmans, 2008).

[31] For a biblical defense of the deity of Christ, see Christopher W. Morgan and Robert A. Peterson, eds., *The Deity of Christ* (Wheaton, IL: Crossway, 2011).

[32] For a recent treatment of the Spirit's deity, personhood, and work, framed in conversation with St. Augustine, St. Thomas Aquinas, and Karl Barth, see

the New Testament make it clear that these three are not simply three modes or manifestations of a unipersonal God, but do indeed represent three distinct persons who exist in relation to one another (Matt 3:13–17; 28:18–20; 2 Cor 13:14).

The New Testament holds in tension the oneness of God, on the one hand, and the coequality of the Father, Son, and Holy Spirit, on the other. It maintains both the unity of the Godhead and the distinctions of the three divine persons. The great fourth-century theologian Gregory of Nazianzus expressed this dynamic well:

> No sooner do I conceive of the One than I am illumined by the Splendor of the Three; no sooner do I distinguish Them than I am carried back to the One. When I think of any One of the Three I think of Him as the Whole, and my eyes are filled, and the greater part of what I am thinking of escapes me. I cannot grasp the greatness of That One so as to attribute a greater greatness to the Rest. When I contemplate the Three together, I see but one torch, and cannot divide or measure out the Undivided Light.[33]

The doctrine of the Trinity was developed over the first four centuries precisely in order to demonstrate how both sides of this biblical mystery—unity and distinction—could be explicated and defended against heterodox views.[34] The doctrine of the Trinity does not so much solve the mystery of the "Undivided Light" as it gives us the proper grammar needed to speak of it truly and reverentially.

Christopher R. J. Holmes, *The Holy Spirit*, New Studies in Dogmatics, ed. Michael Allen and Scott R. Swain (Grand Rapids, MI: Zondervan, 2015).

[33] Gregory of Nazianzus, *Orations* 40.41, in Nicene and Post-Nicene Fathers, 2nd series, vol. 7, *Cyril of Jerusalem, Gregory Nazianzen*, ed. Henry Wace and Philip Schaff (Oxford: James Parker, 1894; Peabody, MA: Hendrickson, 1996).

[34] As Khaled Anatolios points out, Michel Barnes and Lewis Ayres frame their interpretations of the fourth-century debates around the categories of "sameness" and "difference." Anatolios, *Retrieving Nicaea*, 29 n. 41.

In what follows, we will explore three pairings of doctrines that serve as the coordinates for the classical model of the Trinity as we understand it. Each pairing attempts to hold in tension both the sameness and the difference of the Divine Persons.

I. One Nature / Three Persons

II. One Will / Three Modes of Subsistence

III. Inseparable Operations / Appropriation

As we proceed, it should become apparent that each of the elements in the methodology sketched in the first part of the essay has a part to play: exegesis, canonical context, creedal affirmations, and dogmatic considerations. But it should also be obvious that these elements are not to be understood as discrete steps in an irreversible order. In a sense, all of the elements are involved at each step in the process. This is akin to the famous hermeneutical circle, which conceptualizes interpretation as a dialectic between the whole and the parts and between our preunderstandings and the text itself.[35]

I. One Nature / Three Persons

The classical doctrine of the Trinity historically has been expressed in two key terms: person and nature (or essence). The Baptist Catechism expresses succinctly the classical view:

Q. How many persons are there in the Godhead?

A. There are three *persons* in the Godhead, the Father, the Son, and the Holy Spirit; and these three are *one God, the same in essence*, equal in power and glory.[36]

---

[35] For an evangelical appropriation of this principle applied to biblical hermeneutics, see Grant R. Osborne, *The Hermeneutical Spiral: A Comprehensive Introduction to Biblical Interpretation* (Downers Grove, IL: IVP Academic, 2006).

[36] "The Baptist Catechism (Keach's Catechism)," accessed November 29, 2016, http://baptiststudiesonline.com/wp-content/uploads/2007/02/keachs -catechism-of-1677.pdf. Emphasis ours.

So this is the basic grammar of the Trinity: one nature/essence and three persons. But what precisely do these terms signify, and how are they to be distinguished? The classical understanding of these terms is bound up with the controversies of the all-important fourth century. So rather than beginning from modern notions of person and nature, it seems better to retrieve and reiterate the pro-Nicene, orthodox consensus that emerged from the fourth century and was subsequently received and passed on throughout the patristic, medieval, and Reformation eras.[37]

In many ways, the trinitarian debates of the fourth century were disputes over terminology. The story of the emergence of the orthodox consensus, enshrined in the Nicene-Constantinopolitan Creed of 381, is complex. It involves theological and linguistic developments over time, distinctive emphases even among the orthodox parties, and speaking in diverse tongues, as it were (principally, Greek and Latin). But in the end a terminological consensus was reached. The church would come to speak of the Trinity in the following terms:

	Greek	Latin	English Equivalent
Sameness	*ousia*	*Substantia*	Nature/essence/ being
Difference	*hypostasis/prosopon*	*Persona*	person

---

[37] We use the terms "classical," "traditional," and "pro-Nicene" interchangeably in this chapter. This is not intended to paper over the important distinctives and nuances that can be discerned in the trinitarianisms of, say, Athanasius, John of Damascus, Thomas Aquinas, and John Calvin. But we are convinced that there is a coherent and consistent tradition that runs from the pro-Nicenes in the fourth century through the medieval and Reformation eras and beyond. Much of the so-called trinitarian revival of the twentieth century has very little to do with this classical tradition, as Stephen Holmes has shown. See Holmes, *The Quest for the Trinity.*

The decision to settle on *hypostasis* as a reference to the distinct persons was especially significant. The term had previously been seen as a virtual synonym of *ousia* and a rough equivalent of the Latin *substantia*. At Nicaea in 325, speaking of the Father and Son as distinct *hypostases* was explicitly anathematized. But, under the influence of Basil of Caesarea and following a previous council held in Athanasius's Alexandria in 362, the Council of Constantinople sufficiently redefined the term *hypostasis* to signify the three persons and thus removed the anathema against speaking of distinct *hypostases*. The final consensus was: one *ousia*, three *hypostases*.[38]

But what did these terms signify? If there was an agreement of terms, what was the content of that agreement? As noted in the English equivalents above, we can say that the one *ousia* of the Godhead signifies the nature, essence, or being of God. Khaled Anatolios has argued that what bound the orthodox parties of the fourth century together, despite their distinctive emphases, was their understanding of the unity of God in terms of a unity of being. The heterodox parties had tended to understand the Trinity in terms of a unity of will, with the three *hypostases* constituting distinct beings, bound together by the Father's will.[39]

When the pro-Nicenes spoke of the *ousia* of God they meant to connote the being of the Godhead—the infinite, metaphysically simple divine being shared equally by the Father, Son, and Holy Spirit from all eternity. Though creatures can distinguish between divine attributes in terms of our "mode of signification" (*modus significandi*)—to use the language of the medieval Scholastics—these attributes do not map onto distinct *parts* of God's nature—the thing signified (*res significata*). Instead, we are to understand God's nature as one and simple, with each of the attributes mutually informing the others as God

[38] See Anatolios, *Retrieving Nicaea*, 1–31.
[39] Anatolios, 33–79.

reveals himself to creatures.[40] Furthermore, in the traditional under-standing, the divine mind and will are also located, so to speak, in the one divine nature. More accurately, mind and will are distinct ways of signifying the one divine *ousia*. Thus, the pro-Nicene theologians con-sistently affirmed that there is in God one will, one wisdom, one power, and one authority.[41] As Stephen Holmes concludes, the orthodox in both the East and the West insisted "on the unity of the divine will and knowledge."[42]

So the *ousia* connotes what the three divine persons share in com-mon: the simple, ineffable divine essence, which creatures signify in terms of the divine attributes, the divine mind, and the divine will. This *ousia* is not some fourth thing in addition to the three persons, but is instead the being that each person is—the divine nature they share in common from all eternity. As the Nicene Creed famously affirms, the Son is consubstantial (Greek, *homoousia*,[43] of the "same substance") with the Father.[44]

The *hypostases*, on the other hand, pick out what is distinct about the divine persons: their mode of being. As the tradition developed around the unity of the divine *ousia*, these distinctions came to be spo-ken of exclusively in terms of the persons' eternal relations. Building

---

[40] Some examples of pro-Nicene discussion of simplicity can be found in, for example, Gregory of Nyssa, *Against Eunomius* 1.1.19; and Gregory of Nazianzus, *Second Theological Oration*, 7, and *Third Theological Oration*, 10.

[41] This theme will be explored more in the following section.

[42] Holmes, *Quest for the Trinity*, 145.

[43] Again, the pro-Nicenes thought these phrases were thoroughly in accord with the biblical data; Lewis Ayres quotes Athanasius in *Decr.* 19–23 as saying that *homoousios* was used because it "gathered up the sense of the Scriptures." Ayres, *Nicaea and Its Legacy*, 141.

[44] And while the Creed does not speak of the Holy Spirit as *homoousion* with the other two persons, it does speak of him as "co-worshiped" and "co-glorified" with the Father and Son. See Anatolios, *Retrieving Nicaea*, 27. For his part, Gregory of Nazianzus argued for the application of *homoousios* to the Spirit. See Gregory of Nazianzus, *Orations*, 31.10.

on biblical language that was further developed in the second and third centuries and into the fourth,[45] the pro-Nicene tradition defined the persons in terms of eternal relations of origin: the ingeneracy and paternity of the Father, the eternal generation of the Son, and the eternal procession of the Holy Spirit. Note well that *relation* in this patristic sense does not connote "relationship." It is important not to import modern notions of "person" and "relation" into the ancient trinitarian terms. Equivocation must be avoided on this front. For the pro-Nicenes, person did not equal personality, and relation did not equal relationship.[46] Unlike modern "social" or "relational" trinitarian-isms, the pro-Nicene tradition did not understand the divine persons as distinct, psycho-volitional centers of self-consciousness, engaged in I-Thou relationships with one another. Recall that the pro-Nicene tra-dition affirmed numerically one divine mind and will in the Godhead.[47] So when they spoke of the eternal relations of the divine persons, they had in mind not deliberative inter-personal relationships in the modern sense but simply eternal relations of *origin*—distinct modes of

---

[45] There are numerous avenues down which one could explore this biblical language that the pro-Nicenes felt supported the notion of one God in three dis-tinct *hypostases*. From a historical and hermeneutical perspective, see Matthew Bates, *The Birth of the Trinity: Jesus, God, and Spirit in New Testament and Early Christian Interpretations of the Old Testament* (Oxford: Oxford University Press, 2015). Bates argues that the early Christians read Old Testament passages con-taining two or more speakers as indicative of the different persons within the Godhead, a strategy known as prosopological exegesis.

With respect to an overview of the interpretive strategies of the pro-Nicenes and their opponents, including in relation to *hypostasis*, see Anatolios, *Retrieving Nicaea*; and Ayres, *Nicaea and Its Legacy*.

[46] Holmes makes a similar point about the differences between modern social views and the classical tradition. Holmes, *Quest for the Trinity*, 144. Perhaps the clearest example of this in the pro-Nicenes is Nyssen's concluding para-graphs in "On Not Three Gods."

[47] For example, Nazianzen, *Fifth Theological Oration*, 14: "One is not more & another less God; . . . *nor are they divided in will or parted in power* . . . but the Godhead is undivided in separate persons." Emphasis added.

subsistence in the one divine essence.[48] The language of origin is tied to the biblical names of the divine persons—Father, Son, and Spirit—and the biblical descriptions of their eternal and economic relations.[49] To speak about the eternal generation of the Son, for example, is simply to affirm that the Father is *eternally* the *Father* of the Son, and the Son is *eternally* the *Son* of the Father. As in all father-son relations, there is some kind of communication of being between the divine Father and Son, though we must use caution when describing precisely what this eternal generation looks like. We can say that unlike creaturely paternity and sonship, this trinitarian relation of origin is (a) eternal and (b) internal to the being of God. It is reflexive, in that it does not reproduce a second or third god, and it is eternal in that it never had a beginning. The Father never began to be the Father, and the Son never began to be the Son. The Son's origin from the Father is an eternal and immutable procession from the being of the Father and, as such, it cannot signify any inferiority of being—indeed, it cannot signify any *distinction* of being—on the part of the Son.[50] The same principle applies to the eternal procession or spiration (breathing out) of the Holy Spirit from the Father and the Son.[51] The Spirit eternally proceeds from the common spiration of the Father and Son in such a way that he constitutes a distinct hypostasis but not a distinct being.

Speaking of the distinctions between the divine persons exclusively in terms of these eternal relations of origin has sometimes been called

---

[48] See, for example, Nyssen, *Against Eunomius* 1.1.21, 22, 31, 39.

[49] See Athanasius, *Against the Arians* 1.5.16; Basil, *De Spiritu Sancto* 7.17, 8.19, 9.22, 17.43, 18.14.

[50] A common expression from the pro-Nicenes to articulate this concept is "like begets like." See on Father-Son language, begetting, and "like begets like," Athanasius, *Against the Arians* 1.5.16; 2.14.2, 4; 2.18.34, 37–40, 42; and Nyssen, *Against Eunomius* 1.1.31, 32.

[51] Being the central dogmatic debate in the Great Schism, the literature on the *filioque* (the Western addition of the clause "and the Son" to the Nicene Creed) is obviously massive. One of the classic defenses of the clause can be found in Thomas Aquinas, *Summa Theologica*, 1.36.

into question by evangelical theologians. B. B. Warfield rejected this way of distinguishing the persons because he believed it to imply the subordination of the Son and Spirit to the Father.[52] More recently, several other evangelical theologians have called into question, if not the doctrine itself, at least the biblical basis for its acceptance.[53] Because of this rejection or otherwise attenuation of the relations of origin as the exclusive means of distinguishing the divine persons, it is worth exploring the biblical and theological case for the eternal generation of the Son in more detail. The same hermeneutical principles will apply, *mutatis mutandis*, to the eternal procession of the Holy Spirit.

Excursus: The Eternal Generation of the Son

The first point to be made regarding the eternal relations of origin is that these doctrines are rooted in the biblical text. The pro-Nicene theologians saw the eternal relations as eminently biblical, primarily through the pattern of divine naming throughout Scripture. What else does it mean for one person to be Father and another to be Son than that the first person generates, or communicates his essence to, the second person? Likewise, what else would it mean for the Spirit to be the Spirit *of* the Father and Son than that the Spirit is spirated by Father and Son?

---

[52] B. B. Warfield, "Trinity," in *International Standard Bible Encyclopedia*, ed. James Orr (Chicago: Howard-Severance, 1915), vol. 5. Fred Sanders has formatted a helpful annotated version of Warfield's essay, accessed December 5, 2016: http://scriptoriumdaily.com/wp-content/uploads/2015/10/Warfield-Trinity-Study-Edition.pdf.

[53] See, for example, Grudem, *Systematic Theology*, 1234; and Ware, *Father, Son, and Holy Spirit*, 162 n. 3. Both Grudem and Ware have recently affirmed their commitment to the eternal relations of origin, but only in conjunction with their proposed "eternal relations of authority and submission." Whether or not these two ways of distinguishing the persons—relations of origin and relations of authority/submission—can be brought together in a coherent way remains to be discussed below.

Once again we find that this doctrine—this linchpin of Nicene orthodoxy—is grounded in the biblical text. God the Father is not known primarily as "Unoriginate," as Eunomius tried to insist;[54] instead, he is known by the personal and relational name *Father*. In Scripture's analogical language, the fatherhood of the Father is explicated in several texts. Of particular historical and theological importance is Proverbs 8, which speaks of God generating (Hebrew, *qanah*; LXX, *ktizo*) his Wisdom before the creation of the world and then creating all things through this Wisdom (a passage that is reminiscent of John 1:1–4 and Col 1:15–18). Modern scholars have called into question the traditional Christological interpretation of this text, choosing instead to interpret the passage only in terms of its immediate horizon, namely, as a literary device that personifies divine wisdom. But given the New Testament's identification of divine wisdom with Jesus Christ (e.g., 1 Cor 1:24), it is unlikely that Proverbs 8 would be speaking of some Wisdom in God other than the Second Person. This interpretation could even approach positing a fourth "person" active in creation.[55] It is more appropriate, given the canonical context of Proverbs 8, to read this passage as a reference to the Son as the Word and Wisdom of God, eternally generated from the Father before the creation of the world.[56]

Another important text regarding eternal generation is John 5:26.[57] In this passage, Jesus says, ". . . as the Father has life in himself,

---

[54] On this, see Ayres, *Nicaea and Its Legacy*, 144–49, especially 146.

[55] The pro-Nicenes continually make this same point. See, for example, Athanasius, *Against the Arians* 1.2.4, 2.14.5 (one could read only Discourse 2 for this point); Basil, *De Spiritu Sancto* 8.19; Nyssen, *Against Eunomius* 1.22, 24; and Nazianzen, *Fourth Theological Oration*, 2.

[56] For more on this, see Matthew Y. Emerson, "The Role of Proverbs 8: Eternal Generation and Hermeneutics Ancient and Modern," in *Retrieving Eternal Generation*, ed. Fred Sanders and Scott R. Swain (Grand Rapids, MI: Zondervan Academic, 2017).

[57] See Ayres, *Nicaea and Its Legacy*, 152.

so he has granted the Son also to have life in himself." It is clear from the context that the Son is speaking of his equality with the Father in his divinity—specifically in the actions of judging and raising the dead. Even if we were to maintain that Jesus is expressing how these characteristics work themselves out in his incarnate state, John 5:26 is clearly speaking to a reality that transcends Christ's human experience. In other words, the phrase "life in himself" is hard to maneuver toward the incarnation. What would it mean for the Son *qua* human to possess "life in himself"? More than that, what would it mean for the Son *qua* human to possess life in himself *as the Father has life in himself?* It makes little sense to tie this attribute to the Son's incarnate mission. It makes more sense, especially given the context, to understand "life in himself" as a divine attribute that cannot, properly speaking, be granted to any finite creation (that is to say, it is an incommunicable attribute). On this understanding, then, we are forced to understand this "life in himself" and this "granting" of it to the Son in terms of the eternal self-communication that constitutes the immanent Father-Son relation.[58]

A third biblical justification for the eternal relations of origin can be found in the *sentness* of Son and Spirit. As Fred Sanders has argued, the fact that the Son and Spirit are sent in the economy indicates something about their relationship with the Father in the immanent life of the Trinity. As he says, "That eternal relation in God's own being must be, at the very least, a principle of distinctness, since all is one in God except where there is an opposition of relation. But it must be more. It must be some going-forth from God to God in God; some eternal, internal procession. It must be some kind of proceeding of God from God that results in unimaginably perfect unity rather than

---

[58] A version of this paragraph is taken from https://secundumscripturas .com/2016/06/29/a-summarized-biblical-case-for-eternal-generation/.

scattering diversity."[59] In other words, the economic missions are not identical with the immanent processions, but they do proceed from and extend the processions in the economy of redemption. There is a certain fittingness to the missions given the eternal processions. We must be careful not to collapse the missions into the processions, as if everything that obtained in the former (such as submission) must also obtain in the latter. We will deal with this misstep in due course, but for now it is sufficient to note that the sentness of Son and Spirit provides an economic analog, pointing back, as it were, to their eternal relations of origin.

The most obvious biblical warrant for eternal generation, though, can be found in the divine self-naming. "Father," "Son," and "Spirit" tell us not only that these three persons are in relation to one another, but also *how* the three persons relate to one another. The Father exists as Father, that is, as one who has fathered, and the Son exists as Son, that is, as one who is generated. The Holy Spirit, likewise, exists as the Spirit of those who spirate him—Father and Son. While some may posit that the names "Father," "Son," and "Spirit" do not necessarily indicate relations of origin, one wonders what an alternative explanation might be.

It will not do to take these divine names as indicating some sort of ontological hierarchy, as Eunomius and Arius, among others, attempted to do. But neither should we understand these names in terms of an eternal *functional* hierarchy. The assumption of some evangelical theologians is that the names "Father" and "Son" necessitate some kind of eternal relation of authority and submission (ERAS, as it is sometimes abbreviated). These theologians are quick to point

[59] Fred Sanders, "The Sent God," Scriptorium Daily, September 18, 2016, accessed September 29, 2016, http://scriptoriumdaily.com/the-sent-god/. See also Sanders's book on the Trinity: Sanders, *The Triune God* (Grand Rapids: Zondervan, 2016).

out that the authority and submission in question are functional, not ontological. On this view, the Son is equal to the Father in being but willingly submits to him from all eternity, even as a human son should submit to his father.

But there are several problems with this view. Most fundamentally, ERAS seeks to distinguish the persons, not only in terms of their eternal relations of origin, but also in terms of additional properties related to authority and submission. But in the traditional doctrine of the Trinity, the persons share every property in common except for these relations of origin. To add to these traditional distinctions is to introduce a host of theological problems. If the persons are distinguished in terms of their relative authority in the Godhead, then in what sense do they share a common essence, since authority has traditionally been understood as an attribute of the shared divine nature, not a property of the persons? If the persons differ in authority, in what sense can we say that they are coequal? Does the Father stand in a higher position of authority over creation than the Son or Spirit does, since they are eternally and immutably submissive to his authority? Even if one could argue that "Son" implies submission (a proposition difficult to maintain even with human adult sons), how does the language of "Spirit" communicate anything about submission? Furthermore, if the persons are distinguished in terms of authority and submission, does this not require distinct wills in the Godhead? How can one person submit to another unless he possesses some kind of distinct volitional equipment, as it were?[60] Given these problems, it seems that the cost of adding ERAS to the traditional personal distinctions is simply too high. ERAS is neither demanded by Scripture (most of its proof texts fail to account adequately for the practice of partitive exegesis, as will be discussed below) nor is it consistent with the historical position on the eternal personal distinctions.

---

[60] We will return to the problem of the divine will in the next section.

One Will / Three Modes of Subsistence

To this point we have sought to explicate the main terminological apparatus of the doctrine of the Trinity: one nature/essence and three persons. The divine essence (*ousia*) designates what the three persons share in common: the infinite, simple, and ineffable being of God. The three persons (*hypostases*), then, are distinguished only in terms of their eternal relations of origin: the unbegotten Father, the eternally begotten Son, and the eternally proceeding Holy Spirit. Far from constituting speculative impositions on the biblical text, these concepts grow organically from Scripture—not just in terms of one or two proof texts but in terms of broader canonical patterns of biblical language.

So God is one in terms of his essential being, but three in terms of the eternal relations of origin that constitute the three divine persons. The remaining sets of doctrines that we will discuss simply spell out in more detail this key trinitarian distinction. In this section we return to the question of the divine will and explore how the singularity of the divine will is to be held in tension with the three distinct modes of subsistence in it.

As noted above, the traditional doctrine of the Trinity has maintained that the three persons share one divine will. One of the chief problems with the ERAS position is that it stands in some tension with this belief in the unity of the divine will. We are using "will" here to denote a volitional *faculty*, not merely a shared desire, plan, or intention. It is an ontological reality, not merely a functional one. In the latter, weaker sense, the Arians and Eunomians could have affirmed the unity of the divine will—and, indeed, they did.[61] But in this stronger, ontological sense, the unity of the divine will is explained in terms of the divine essence or being. The will is a faculty of the shared *ousia*, not a property distinct to the three *hypostases*. So perhaps it is more accurate to speak not only of the *unity* of the divine will (which could imply

---

[61] See on this especially Anatolios, *Retrieving Nicaea*, 41–79.

nothing more than the harmony of three discrete wills) but also of the *singularity* of the divine will. Just as there is numerically one divine essence, so there is numerically one divine will.

The pro-Nicene Fathers were united in their insistence on this singularity of the divine will. Commenting on John 6:38 ("For I have come down from heaven, not to do my own will but the will of him who sent me"), Gregory of Nazianzus writes,

> But since, as this is the language of him who assumed our nature (for he it was who came down), and not of the nature which he assumed, we must meet the obligation in this way, that the passage does not mean that the Son has a special will of his own, besides that of the Father, but that he has not; so that the meaning would be, "Not to do mine own will, for there is none of mine apart from, but that which is common to, me and thee; for as we have one Godhead, so we have one will."[62]

Gregory is practicing here what we have already referred to as *partitive exegesis*: the common patristic strategy of determining whether a biblical passage is speaking of the Son of God in terms of his deity or in terms of his humanity. Gregory notes that this particular text (John 6:38) is speaking of the person of the Son ("him who assumed our nature"), and not of the Son in his incarnate state ("the nature which he assumed"). Understood in this way, this text could be interpreted as positing distinct divine wills: the will of the Father who sends and the will of the Son who comes down from heaven. So John 6:38 is sometimes adduced to defend some version of ERAS. But interestingly, Gregory does not read the text in this fashion. Instead, he understands Jesus to be speaking by way of negation. It is impossible for the Son to seek some private will distinct from the Father's precisely because the two persons share the same will, which inheres in their shared

---

[62] Gregory of Nazianzus, *Orations*, 30.12.

Godhead. So, again, Gregory paraphrases Jesus's saying: "Not to do mine own will, for there is none of mine apart from, but that which is common to, me and thee; for as we have one Godhead, so we have one will." For Gregory, wills belong to natures, and since there is but one divine nature, there can be but one divine will.

The other pro-Nicene Fathers agreed with Nazianzen on this point. Gregory's compatriot Gregory of Nyssa argued similarly that the will is a property of the divine essence. Arguing against Eunomius's view that the Father and Son are distinct beings because they are engaged in distinct workings (*energeia*), Nyssen writes, "For if there existed any variation in their energies, so that the Son worked His will in a different manner to the Father then (on the above supposition) it would be fair to conjecture, from this variation, a variation also in the beings which were the result of these varying energies."[63]

But, as Nyssen demonstrates, there is no variation in the workings of Father, Son, and Spirit. They are each inseparably at work in creation and redemption. Since there is no variation in their energies, there can be no variation in their being. For Nyssen, no less than Nazianzen, the will and working of the divine persons are one, not many. While these are only two passages that affirm the singularity of the divine will, there are many more that we could cite to make the same point: God is one in every way (the relations of origin excepted), including in his volitional faculty.[64]

This pro-Nicene position on the singularity of the divine will is consistent with subsequent orthodoxy as well. To pick just one

---

[63] Gregory of Nyssa, *Against Eunomius*, 1.27.

[64] For example, Nazianzen, *Second Theological Oration*, 7, and *Third Theological Oration*, 10; Athanasius, *Against the Arians*, 3.25.10; Basil, *De Spiritu Sancto*, 8.20–21, 18.45; Nyssen, "On the Holy Trinity," passim; Nyssen, "On 'Not Three Gods,'" passim; and Nyssen, *Against Eunomius* 1.1.19, 21, 27, 34. And, lest one think that the pro-Nicenes's affirmation of unity in "power" is distinct from their unity of volitional faculty, Nyssen actually heads off this argument in *Against Eunomius* 1.1.28, 31, as does Nazianzen in *Fifth Theological Oration*, 14.

representative example, many centuries later John Calvin would explicitly affirm the singularity of the divine will in his commentary on the Gethsemane narrative: "This passage shows plainly enough the gross folly of those ancient heretics, who were called *Monothelites*, because they imagined that the will of Christ was but one and simple; for Christ, as he was God, *willed* nothing different from the Father; and therefore, it follows, that his human soul had affections distinct from the secret purpose of God."[65]

Note that Calvin understands the agony of Christ in the Garden in terms of his human soul, not in terms of his divine nature. As God, the person of the Son "willed nothing different from the Father." It is only as man that the Son possesses a will distinct from the Father. Even then, the human will of Christ was perfectly conformed to the divine will. According to Calvin, Christ genuinely "felt, without being wounded by them, those temptations which pierce us with their stings" and yet "remained firm and unshaken" in the face of temptation.[66] So Christ's human will is aligned with the divine will in furtherance of his mission as humanity's representative and substitute. But in terms of his divinity, the Son wills precisely what the Father wills because they share the common will of the divine essence.

But how can the three persons act and relate to one another if there is only one divine will? Some might wonder, does the affirmation of one divine will not run the risk of modalism, with the three persons merely distinct manifestations or revelations of God but not truly distinct *hypostases*? How are we to understand eternal relations of love within the Godhead, if God is reduced to a single psycho-volitional subject? This seems to be the concern of some proponents of ERAS. In some ways, we believe this objection begs the question. Since God is *sui*

---

[65] John Calvin, *A Commentary on A Harmony of the Evangelists: Matthew, Mark, and Luke*, trans. William Pringle, Calvin's Commentaries (Grand Rapids, MI: Baker, 2003), 3:233. Emphasis added.

[66] Calvin, 3:233.

generis (no other *ousia* is supposited by three distinct *hypostases*), how are we to know what must be the case in order for the three persons to relate to one another? It seems to us that a healthy dose of apophaticism is in order when it comes to reflecting on and speaking about God's inner life.[67] Indeed, this is one of the reasons we believe it is a mistake to draw too close a connection between the Trinity and any human social relation, as both proponents and critics of ERAS have been prone to do with human gender relations.[68]

We can say that while there is only one divine will, there are three modes of subsistence (or existence) in that one will.[69] So the three relate to one another in ways appropriate to their eternal relations of origin, but we are not to understand these relations as a function of some volitional equipment behind the shared, singular divine will. Instead, these modes of subsistence *just are* the distinct relations of origin. The will of the Father generates but is not distinct from the will of the Son. The shared will of the Father and Son spirates but is not distinct from the will of the Spirit. The will is identical, but the three persons subsist in it according to their distinct personal modes. This

---

[67] On this point, see the important essay by Karen Kilby, "Is an Apophatic Trinitarianism Possible?" *IJST* 12, no. 1 (January 2010): 65–77.

[68] The literature on this precise question is voluminous and, in many ways, misguided, in our view. There are social trinitarians on either side of the complementarian-egalitarian debate, and there are traditional (Latin) trinitarians on either side as well. So, it seems to us that the best way forward is to decouple the Trinity debate from the gender debate. The most commonly cited text from the complementarian side is 1 Cor 11:3, "But I want you to understand that the head of every man is Christ, the head of a wife is her husband, and the head of Christ is God." But partitive exegesis is necessary here as well: this text is speaking of the Son in his incarnate state and says nothing directly about the Son's immanent relation to the Father. For an entry point to these issues, see Dennis W. Jowers and H. Wayne House, eds., *The New Evangelical Subordinationism? Perspectives on the Equality of God the Father and God the Son* (Eugene, OR: Pickwick, 2012).

[69] Thomas Aquinas speaks of persons as rational subsistences in that "they exist in themselves and not in another." Aquinas, *Summa Theologica*, 1.29.2.

view should not be confused with *modalism,* however.[70] The persons are distinct modes of *subsistence,* not merely distinct modes of *revelation.* The persons are constituted by really existing relations of "opposition" in the Godhead.[71]

Defenders of the classical Reformed doctrine of the *pactum salutis,* or covenant of redemption, have appealed to this distinction between one will and three modes of subsistence in order to demonstrate how there can be an eternal "agreement" between persons who share the same will. In a recent defense of the *pactum,* Reformed theologian Scott Swain points to the reflections of seventeenth-century theologians John Owen and Wilhelmus à Brakel to demonstrate the coherency of this doctrine. Both Owen and à Brakel affirm the singularity of the divine will, but also speak about "distinct applications" of (Owen) or distinct "perspective[s]" on (à Brakel) this one divine will, corresponding to the distinct modes of subsistence in it. Swain concludes, "In other words, when it comes to the relationship between the pactum salutis and the divine will, we must consider not only that will's unity and indivisibility, we must also consider that will's tripersonal manner of subsistence if we are to appreciate the doctrine's status as an instance of orthodox trinitarian reasoning."[72] So God's will is singular, but this singularity does not erase the real distinctions that exist between the three modes of subsistence in the one divine will.

---

[70] In another context, Moltmann levels a similar criticism against Rahner's understanding of the persons as "modes of subsistence." Jurgen Moltmann, *The Trinity and the Kingdom: The Doctrine of God* (Minneapolis, MN: Fortress, 1993), 146–48.

[71] Aquinas speaks of the relations in the Godhead in terms of "real opposition" in order to highlight that the persons are really distinct, not with regard to the shared divine essence, but relative to their personal properties. Aquinas, *Summa Theologica,* 1.29.3.

[72] Scott R. Swain, "Covenant of Redemption," in *Christian Dogmatics: Reformed Theology for the Church Catholic,* ed. Michael Allen and Scott R. Swain (Grand Rapids, MI: Baker Academic, 2016), 117–18.

Inseparable Operations / Appropriation

We now come to the final pairing of doctrines that hold together the sameness and the difference of the divine persons: inseparable operations and appropriation. The doctrine of inseparable operations is rooted both in Scripture and in the earliest centuries of Christian reflection, but it receives its classical expression from St. Augustine: "According to the Catholic faith, the Trinity is proposed to our belief and believed—and even understood by a few saints and holy persons— as so inseparable that whatever is done by it must be thought to be performed at the same time by the Father and by the Son and by the Holy Spirit."[73]

The doctrine is often framed in terms of the Latin formula, *opera Trinitatis ad extra indivisa sunt* (the external works of the Trinity are undivided). The internal (*ad intra*) relations of God are distinct; indeed, as discussed above, these eternal relations of origin are the *only* properties that distinguish the divine persons. But the external (*ad extra*) works of the Godhead are indivisible.[74] All the external works of God—creation, providence, redemption, judgment, and restoration— are carried out inseparably by all three persons. As we will see below, even when certain trinitarian works are appropriated to one particular member of the Godhead, the indivisibility of God's action remains. So, for example, even though only the Son dies on the cross (and then only by virtue of his human nature, since the Son is immortal in terms

---

[73] Augustine, *Ep.* 11.2, trans. Lewis Ayres, *Augustine and the Trinity* (New York: Cambridge University Press, 2010), 59–60.

[74] This raises an important distinction for classical trinitarianism: the distinction between God's life *ad intra* and his works *ad extra*, between the eternal processions and the economic missions. The Greek Fathers often spoke about this distinction in terms of *theologia* and *economia*. This distinction becomes important for understanding how the Son submits himself to the Father in his economic mission but not in his immanent relation to the Father. The economic missions flow from and reflect the eternal processions, but not everything that obtains in the former can be applied to the latter.

of his divine nature), it is the triune God who inseparably works to bring about redemption through his death.[75] The Father gives up the Son to death (Rom 8:32), the Son lays down his life of his own accord (John 10:18), and he does so through the eternal Spirit (Heb 9:14).

In a sense, the doctrine of inseparable operations is simply a corollary of trinitarian monotheism. If there is one God—one divine essence—then it cannot be the case that the three persons would operate as free agents distinct from one another. As there is one divine essence and one divine will, so there is one divine energy and one divine action in all God's external works. The Scriptures make explicit this unity of action. In John 5:19, Jesus confesses, "Truly, truly, I say to you, the Son can do nothing of his own accord, but only what he sees the Father doing. For whatever the Father does, that the Son does likewise." Two verses later, Jesus expresses the reciprocal nature of this inseparability: "For the Father judges no one, but has given all judgment to the Son, that all may honor the Son, just as they honor the Father. Whoever does not honor the Son does not honor the Father who sent him" (John 5:22–23). Later in John, Jesus makes clear that the Holy Spirit is engaged in this great trinitarian work as well: "He will glorify me, for he will take what is mine and declare it to you. All that the Father has is mine; therefore I said that he will take what is mine and declare it to you" (John 16:14–15).

To be clear, there is an order (Greek, *taxis*) to trinitarian action, which is reflective of the order of the eternal relations of origin. The works of God are carried out from the Father through the Son by the Spirit (see 1 Cor 8:6; Rom 11:36; Col 1:16). But order here does not imply *sub*-order, so to speak. Nor does it imply merely harmonious but ultimately independent action. The ordered work of the Triune remains undivided. As God is one, so are his works.

---

[75] Appropriation is important in this regard in order to avoid Patripassianism, the ancient modalistic heresy that maintained that the Father suffered on the cross.

As noted above, the doctrine of inseparable operations must be held in close connection with the doctrine of appropriation. Appropriation was a common theme in medieval scholasticism and is perhaps most notably associated with Thomas Aquinas. The central idea in appropriation is that we can attribute (*appropriare*) certain names or properties to certain members of Trinity without sundering their essential unity. Nevertheless, as Aquinas explains, "The essential attributes are not appropriated to the persons as if they exclusively belonged to them."[76] It is appropriate to speak of the Father as Creator, the Son as Redeemer, and the Spirit as Sanctifier, but we do so with the understanding that all three persons are engaged in all these divine works. The Son and Spirit are active in creation and providence no less than the Father. The Father and Spirit are active in the work of atonement no less than the Son. And the Father and Son are active in the sanctification and perfection of God's people no less than the Spirit. So, we return once again to the doctrine of inseparable operations: though we may speak of certain actions terminating on certain members of the Trinity, we must acknowledge that all three persons are working indivisibly in all of God's external acts.

Conclusion

We believe that the classical doctrine of the Trinity as articulated in the Nicene-Constantinopolitan Creed and received in the great tradition of Christian theology, across denominational and geographical lines, is an eminently biblical doctrine. The language of the Trinity—one *ousia* and three *hypostases*—may not be found in the pages of holy Scripture, but the judgment that this conceptual apparatus renders is a faithful explication of the biblical teaching on the being and works of the triune God. This is not to say that doctrines such as the eternal

---

[76] Aquinas, *Summa Theologica*, 1.39.7–8.

processions, the singularity of the divine will, and inseparable operations can simply be deduced from a list of proof texts. Instead, as we have argued, when the Scriptures are read carefully as a canonical whole, considering the history of interpretation and guided by biblically grounded doctrines, they give more than adequate support for these classical trinitarian themes. Evangelical theologians need not surrender the precious doctrine of *sola scriptura* in order to appeal to the consensual tradition on these matters. Rather, we humbly suggest that evangelical theology is at its best when it positions itself as a renewal movement within historic Christian orthodoxy, not as an innovating sect pushing the boundaries of orthodoxy.[77] In the end, the doctrine of the Trinity does not present to us a set of abstract ideas, distinct from the God of the Bible and Christian experience. Instead, the doctrine of the Trinity simply provides us with time-tested conceptual language by which we might defend and explicate all that Scripture teaches about God. In this sense, the doctrine of the Trinity is the most practical of all doctrines in that it undergirds all our prayers, all our preaching, all our evangelism, and all our discipleship as we seek to live *coram Deo*—before the face of our great triune God.

---

[77] This has been one of the burdens of Timothy George's immensely helpful work over the years. See especially, Timothy George, ed., *Evangelicals and Nicene Faith: Reclaiming the Apostolic Witness* (Grand Rapids, MI: Baker Academic, 2011).

CHAPTER 4

Response to Malcolm B. Yarnell III, Matthew Y. Emerson, and Luke Stamps

By Bruce A. Ware

I'm grateful for the careful, thoughtful, and diligent work represented by these fine chapters. As I read these contributions, I found myself in agreement with most of what these authors have presented and argued. Perhaps it would be fitting to begin with select areas of agreement before moving to some points of difference.

On Malcolm Yarnell's chapter, I affirm with him the main points he articulates, as summarized in the introduction to the chapter. He, perhaps controversially, affirms the connection between the creation of man as male and female in the image of God and the unity and plurality within the Trinity. I affirm with him that this link is intended by the author of Genesis, particularly in the way he crafts his discussion of image of God in Gen 1:26–28. Yarnell writes, "We do not find any reason to doubt the general claim that relations within God are

129

the basis for the male-female relation and thence all relations within
humanity. With the premodern theologians and with many theologians since Bonhoeffer's formulation, we find the *imago Dei* reflects
God in his singular and relational reality" (p. 88). To my mind, the
deliberate introduction of the plural language regarding the one
God in Gen 1:26 ("Let us," "our image," and "our likeness") followed
by the references to his human creation in both singular and plural
terms ("man," "him," along with "them" and "male and female") are
intended to draw a connection between the one God who is plural
and the one human creation who likewise is plural. And when one
sees in the early chapters of Genesis both the full equality of the man
and woman, along with the headship of the man in this relationship
(witness Paul's appeal to features of Genesis 2–3 supporting male
headship in 1 Cor 11:7–9 and 1 Tim 2:12–15), it seems to me an altogether legitimate reading of this text. The author of Genesis intends
that we see the link between unity and plurality in God "imaged" in
the unity and plurality of *imago Dei* man, created male and female. Of
course, much more needs to be said to make a full case for this interpretation, but suffice it to say that I believe Yarnell is on the right track
in his discussion.

Regarding the Emerson-Stamps chapter, I affirm much of what
they argue in laying out a pro-Nicene understanding of the Trinity. I
also affirm the methodology they encourage readers to use in formulating and evaluating a trinitarian understanding. I affirm with them
the trinitarian formulations of the early councils of the church, including the affirmation of the Son as eternally begotten from the Father,
and the Spirit eternally proceeding from the Father and the Son (following the Western inclusion of the *filioque*). I also appreciate the
description they provided of the methodology they urged readers to
consider. This methodology considers broad historical and contextual
features along with direct appeal to scriptural texts. As with much else,
the devil is in the details. We must all watch carefully to ensure that full
consideration is given to biblical texts in a manner that demonstrates

sola Scriptura. But in principle, I agree with Emerson and Stamps on their methodological claims.

My differences come largely with Emerson and Stamps's criticism of the legitimacy of ERAS, and I will devote the remainder of my response to questions they raised here. In the main, they object that the existence of both eternal relations of origin and eternal relations of authority and submission in the triune Godhead introduces a second basis for distinguishing the divine persons. They, on the other hand, prefer to argue that "in the traditional doctrine of the Trinity, the persons share every property in common except for these relations of origin" (p. 118). I affirm that the only ontological distinction among the trinitarian persons is their eternal relations of origin. Father is distinguished ontologically because he exists eternally as unbegotten or ingenerate; the Son's ontological distinction appears in being eternally begotten of the Father; and the Spirit's ontological distinction appears in eternally proceeding from the Father and the Son. Yet as unbegotten, begotten, and proceeding, the three trinitarian persons each possess fully the numerically identical divine nature and hence each is equally and fully God. While all in the pro-Nicene tradition to which Emerson and Stamps refer affirm this, at least some notable figures in this same tradition have seen that this unique ontological distinction entails an accompanying functional or operational distinction which also may rightly be included to distinguish the persons from one another.

Charles Hodge, for example, speaks of a subordination among the trinitarian persons with regard both to their respective mode of subsistence and to their respective mode of operation. The former is ontological, whereas the latter is functional. He writes,

> Subordination as to the mode of subsistence and operation, is a Scriptural fact; and so also is the perfect and equal Godhead of the Father and the Son, and therefore these facts must be consistent. In the consubstantial identity of the human soul there

is a subordination of one faculty to another, and so, however
incomprehensible to us, there may be a subordination in the
Trinity consistent with the identity of essence in the Godhead.[1]

For Hodge, the persons are coeternal and coequal in deity, yet a subordination in the mode of subsistence is tied directly to a subordination in the mode of operation. In other words, because the Father
begets the Son, it will be the Father who sends the Son and precisely
not the Son sending the Father. Because the Spirit proceeds from the
Father and the Son, the Spirit will be sent by the Father and the Son
rather than sending either the Father or the Son. One distinction is
ontological; the other functional. Yet both are eternally true since the
operational subordination is expressive of the ontological mode of
subsistence.

James Petigru Boyce strengthens the operational subordination
of the Son to the Father, arguing it is even "more plainly" taught in
Scripture. Consider his words:

> 3. The personal inferiority [of the Son to the Father, and of
> the Spirit to the Father and the Son] which is thus made pos-
> sible, so far as it is natural, is due doubtless to the difference
> in the modes of subsistence . . . In this mode of subsistence,
> therefore, inferiority of the person of the Son to the Father,
> and of the Spirit to the Father and Son, may be said to exist.
> Without any superiority as God, therefore, the Father may be
> said to be greater than the Son, because of the personal rela-
> tions in the Trinity.

> 4. But there is also a subordination of office or rank still more
> plainly taught. By virtue of this, the Father sends the Son, and

---

[1] Charles Hodge, *Systematic Theology* (Grand Rapids, MI: Eerdmans, 1979),
1.474. For further discussion of Hodge's appeal to "mode of subsistence and
operation," see also his discussion on pp. 460–62.

the Father and Son send the Spirit. This could exist between persons in all respects equal to each other, both in nature and relation. In God, however, it is probable that the official subordination [i.e., subordination in office] is based upon that of the personal relations [i.e., modes of subsistence in the divine being]. It corresponds exactly with the relations of the persons, from which has probably resulted their official subordination in works without, and especially in the work of redemption.

The order of this subordination is plainly apparent from the scriptural names and statements about the relations. The Father is unquestionably first, the Son second, and the Holy Spirit third. This is their rank, as well because of the mode of subsistence, as of its order. Hence they are commonly spoken of in this order, as the First, Second and Third Persons of the Trinity.[2]

As with Hodge, Boyce likewise affirms the complete and unqualified equality of the three trinitarian persons in full deity while also distinguishing them in terms of "official subordination" as well as "personal relations," with the former probably tied to and expressive of the latter.

One might quibble over whether we have only one distinction among the trinitarian persons, or two. One could easily argue that only one is fundamental: the eternal relations of origin. But so long as it is the case that the "operational" or "official" subordination of Son to the Father, and of the Spirit to the Father and the Son, flows from the eternal relations of origin, both need to be acknowledged as true. Call them one distinction with two expressions, or two distinctions, we still have two subjects to discuss when raising the question of what distinguishes the Father, Son, and Spirit from one another.

---

[2] James P. Boyce, "Personal Relations in the Trinity," in *Abstract of Systematic Theology*, accessed June 20, 2018, http://www.reformedreader.org/rbb/boyce /aos/chapter15.htm.

Emerson and Stamps raise a related issue, discussing whether affirming eternal relations of authority and submission to the trinitarian persons compromises the equality of essence shared fully and equally by the Father, and the Son, and the Spirit. Would not attributing a distinctive paternal authority to the Father and a distinctive filial submission to the Son indicate that they do not possess the same nature? Allow me a few brief responses. First, a central question here is whether "authority" and "submission" are properties of one's nature, or whether they are relational properties that exist between or among persons. I argued in my own chapter that they are the latter. I won't here repeat what I've said already, except to note if we insist authority is an attribute of one's nature, and if we agree one may have authority one day but lose it the next day, we would have to conclude the person's nature changed when they were granted authority they did not have previously, or were divested of authority they had just had. Yet we know that this is not the case. Both authority and submission are properties of personal relationships and not of one's nature.

Second, the fact that the trinitarian persons are named Father, Son, and Spirit indicates there is something built into the respective identities of these three distinct persons. They are not brother-brother-brother, friend-friend-friend, or God-clone-clone. Hilary saw this when he wrote, "Having a name which belongs to Him whose Son He is, He is subject to the Father both in service and name; yet in such a way that the subordination of His name bears witness to the true character of His natural and exactly similar essence."[3] So what does "Son" indicate? Two things, says Hilary: his full equality with the Father in nature and his hypostatic subjection to the Father. The Son holds both because he is the Son of the Father. Within biblical revelation, the language used to describe relations between Father, Son, and Spirit especially

---

[3] Hilary of Poitiers (ca. 300–368), *On the Councils* 51, A Select Library of Nicene and Post-Nicene Fathers of the Christian Church, ed. Philip Schaff, 2nd series, vol. 9 (Grand Rapids, MI: Eerdmans, 1952–57), 18–19.

confirms this. Why is the Father always the one who directs, sends, commissions, decrees, and purposes, in relation to the Son and to the Spirit? Is it not because he is Father? Jonathan Edwards saw this when he wrote, "That the economy of the persons of the Trinity, establishing that order of their acting that is agreeable to the order of their subsisting, is entirely diverse from the covenant of redemption, and prior to it, not only appears from the nature of things, but appears evidently from the Scripture."[4] For Edwards, this order of acting is built into the trinitarian relations as "agreeable to their order of subsisting." This is vitally important and raises my third response.

Third, if the relations of authority and submission so very evident among the trinitarian persons are not eternal, then we have a problem. We must say that these relations began. But when? And why do they begin in the manner that we see expressed in Scripture? And what do we say about the immutability of the God who has revealed himself displaying paternal authority and filial submission?

Do these relations of authority and submission begin, as some insist, only in the incarnation? This just cannot be. It makes a mockery of the Father's sending of the Son, his motive of love, and his purpose to save, that he—the Father—has willed in his Son. It also fails to account for the submission of the Spirit to the Son, where the Spirit is not the subject of some incarnational condescension (John 16:13–14). Well then, does the relation of authority and submission begin in the *pactum salutis?* Certainly, this accounts for the economic Trinity's works *ad extra,* but it does not account for our second question. Why do they begin (if they do so begin) the way they do?

It seems to me one must say with Edwards that the order of acting, which indeed is agreeable to the order of subsisting, is "entirely diverse from" and "prior to" the covenant of redemption. Indeed, the way in which the covenant of redemption is structured expresses the eternal

---

[4] Edwards, "Economy of the Trinity and Covenant of Redemption," *WJE* 20:1062.

relations of origin, which themselves express the eternal relations of
authority and submission that derive from the hypostatic identities of
Father, Son, and Spirit.

And what do we conclude if the revelation of the trinitarian God
depicts himself always and only as possessing paternal authority and
filial submission and yet we propose that this is not true of the eternal
God? Here I ask two questions in reply: (1) Why would you doubt
that the revelation of God is truly the revelation of the eternal and
immutable God? Since authority and submission are seen in trinitarian relations not only in the incarnation but in the whole sweep of
God's revelation of himself to us, it seems only right to accept this
is indeed descriptive of God. (2) If you propose God eternally is not
what he has revealed himself to be, on what possible basis do you claim
to know this? Why should we accept as legitimate a claim that God is
other than that which he has fully and solely revealed himself to be?

One last question will occupy the remaining space of my response.
Does this imply or entail multiple wills in God? Again, I've addressed
this topic in my chapter, and I will not repeat here what I've said
already. But here let me simply note that others in the pro-Nicene
tradition have seen the need for a distinction of hypostatic willing,
while maintaining the one will of the one God. Emerson and Stamps
indicate this themselves when discussing Scott Swain's appeal to Owen
and à Brakel's references to distinct "applications" or "perspectives" of
hypostatic willing (p. 124). Each trinitarian person wills the one will
but in distinctive ways. Consider also an observation made by William
G. T. Shedd on a related subject:

> The Scriptures teach that the Father, Son, and Holy Spirit
> are three persons independently and irrespective of creation,
> redemption, and sanctification. If God had never created the
> universe, but had existed along from all eternity, he would be
> triune. And the three persons are so real and distinct from
> each other, that each possesses a hypostatical or trinitarian

consciousness different from that of the others. The second person is conscious that he is the Son, and not the Father, when he says, "O Father, glorify thou me," John 17:5. The first person is conscious that he is the Father and not the Son, when he says, "Thou art my Son, this day have I begotten thee," Heb 1:5 . . . These three hypostatical consciousnesses constitute the one self-consciousness of the Divine essence. By reason of, and as the result of these three forms of consciousness, the Divine essence is self-contemplative, self-cognitive, and self-communing.[5]

I would suggest that we apply the same kind of logic to the question of the divine will. There is one and only one will in God in terms of volitional capacity of the nature of God and in terms of the content of that will. Yet there must be hypostatically distinct expressions of that will, as when the Father, conscious that he is the Father, wills to say, "Thou art my Son." Of course, presumably the Son would naturally also will to say, "Indeed, I am gladly and eternally thy Son." So the content of the willing of each may be in full agreement and expressive of the same fundamental reality, yet the perspective and hypostatic distinctiveness must also be maintained. Can the Father's authoritative will to send the Son and the Son's submissive will to be sent by the Father be the same will? Yes, indeed. They constitute hypostatically distinct perspectives on the one and same divine will. One divine will along with three real, yet united, hypostatically distinctive volitional expressions of that one will—both are required to account fully for the one God who is genuinely One while he is also genuinely Three.

[5] William G. T. Shedd, *Dogmatic Theology*, 3 vols., 2nd ed. (Nashville: Thomas Nelson, 1980), 1:282.

CHAPTER 5

Response to Bruce A. Ware, Matthew Y. Emerson, and Luke Stamps

By Malcolm B. Yarnell III

One of the greatest joys for any Christian theologian occurs when responding to brothers and sisters in Jesus Christ regarding the wonderful truths God has revealed. It is a privilege to converse with Bruce Ware, Matthew Emerson, and Luke Stamps, along with the editor of our volume, Keith Whitfield. Each has my gratitude for, in this volume and elsewhere, drawing me closer to the Lord. They have blessed me through their careful exegesis of Scripture, helpful review of the biblical exegeses of the historical church, and thoughtful application to the contemporary context. Reading the essays of my fellow contributors reminds me of how I remain in their debt. It also indicates where I do not fall exactly in line with their methods or conclusions, even as I recognize the evangelical commitments of each contributor.

This diversity among Christian evangelicals is a vivid example of how we have a *perfect God*, while we ourselves remain *imperfect theologians*.

My purpose in contributing to this volume was not to stake out a position in the contemporary debates on Trinity and gender. Rather, it was to explore and propose a method for moving from theological discovery to anthropological description. Yes, I am concerned with the Trinity and gender debate, a debate that flared up with renewed intensity in the summer and fall of 2016. However, debating gender relations should come only after discerning a proper way to correlate the doctrine of God with the doctrine of the creature that is made in the image of God. For those dedicated to the Trinity and gender debate, especially in its most recent round, which occurred between fellow complementarians, the essays of the other contributors will doubtless be of greater moment, for they address those issues more pointedly.

That said, the editor asked me to reflect on the other contributions, so it now seems that, yet again, I will be drawn into the discussion. This author's once and continued reluctance to enter the contemporary controversy is not based on any major disagreement regarding outcomes. I remain both trinitarian in theology and complementarian in my understanding of gender relations among human beings, like my colleagues. Rather, this author's reluctance results from a disagreement about method. As my essay makes clear, I think we need to be very careful about combining too closely or transitioning too hastily between our anthropological claims and our doctrine of God. That said, I concede to the editor's request and will respond to a few of the other contributors' claims. We shall consider both methodology and theology.

Methodological Considerations

The other essayists bring forward some important contributions to the discussion of theological method as it pertains to the doctrines of the Trinity and of theological anthropology. Consider the positive methodological contributions made by the other writers:

First, as a fellow biblicist, I wholeheartedly affirm the consistent efforts of Bruce Ware to refer evangelicals of all kinds back to Scripture in order to construct our doctrines. One factor that I have really appreciated about Ware's theological ministry is that he refuses to content himself with mere mimicry of the history of biblical exegesis. While respectfully regarding what he calls the "church's doctrine" and ready to employ the tradition in his theological construction, he is unwilling to hold a doctrine simply because it can be found within the tradition. Like Martin Luther before him, Ware seems ready and willing to confess something if, and only if, he can be reasonably convinced it is based on the Word of God. Every evangelical should be encouraged by Ware's high view of Scripture. And every free churchman should be especially encouraged by his radical application of biblicism. God and his Word alone are perfect.

Second, Matthew Emerson and Luke Stamps have put forward a holistic theological method that I can affirm in large part. Their claim is that determining what is "biblical" doctrine includes being "illumined by the Spirit, rooted in biblical exegesis, governed by patterns of biblical language, shaped by the biblical economy, guided by the biblically derived rule of faith, guarded by biblically derived tradition, refined by systematic and philosophical reflection, and located within the communion of the saints" (pp. 12, 105). In this, they harmonize with many of my own arguments and conclusions, about which I have written extensively.[1] Where Ware reminds us of the need continually to reform our theology through reference to the biblical text, Matthew and Luke remind us that the very act of referral to the biblical text is one that requires the guidance of the Holy Spirit and the context of the church of Jesus Christ.

From a methodological perspective, the only corrections I would deign to offer both essays concern preferred emphases. While I was

---

[1] See Malcolm B. Yarnell III, *The Formation of Christian Doctrine* (Nashville, TN: B&H Academic, 2007).

heartened that Bruce consistently refers to the biblical text, there are times it would have been helpful to seek guidance from relevant exegesis within the tradition. Although Bruce draws on the church fathers, only certain points seem to have been emphasized, rather than the totality of their witness. For instance, research into the doctrine of divine perfection, about which more is said below, might have served particularly well.

As for a critique of Matthew and Luke, I would only argue that they might have earlier noted their rejection of "biblicism" is not a rejection *in toto*. Rather, if I read them correctly, they are rejecting one form of biblicism, which we might call "naïve biblicism," "thin biblicism," or even "fundamentalism." Instead of such truncated use of the Bible, they advocate a "thick biblicism" (p. 11, 97). In summary comparison, we can say that where Bruce is less conversant with the tradition than I, Matthew and Luke are more dependent on tradition than I am. Again, I raise these issues not for contention over substance but for identifying preferences in method. Now we turn to theology, particularly theology proper.

Theological Considerations

While in method I equally appreciate Bruce Ware's thorough biblicism and Matthew Emerson and Luke Stamps's call for the appropriation of tradition, in the doctrine of God I found myself more in line with the conclusions of the latter.[2] This is not to say that I stand in opposition to Bruce's theology proper, but that I have a few questions about his presentation of divine ontology. However, there are important resources available within his writings that indicate this query does not produce a significant variance.

---

[2] It should be clear by this time that the doctrine of humanity is not at issue here.

In the end, the doctrinal questions remain important, even though the four authors in this book may agree on many features of the doctrine of God. Let me begin by addressing three themes from the writings of Bruce Ware regarding the doctrine of God. After identifying these three themes, we shall make three queries regarding the doctrine of God in Bruce's essay in this volume. Finally, we shall propose a way forward.

Ware: Three Themes

The first theme touches on Bruce Ware's constant and correct challenge to reexamine our doctrine of God through returning to Scripture. For instance, earlier in his career, he stated flatly in response to contemporary and longstanding claims about divine immutability, "God's self-revelation must be the sole guide in thinking on this or any other issue relating to who God is."[3] While willing to "reformulate" the doctrine of God according to fresh biblical exegesis, this did not mean he accepted any and all claims for such a reformulation. For instance, later, in controversy with the open theists, he took a strong stand against recasting the orthodox doctrine of divine immanence, for the open theists had significantly strayed from the biblical text.[4]

The second theological theme from Bruce's writings that requires rehearsal concerns the importance of theological metaphysics. While his primary interests in the open theism controversy were divine providence and divine foreknowledge, he also touched on divine ontology. The nature of God was not his principal concern in that earlier controversy, because it dealt with the nearness of God rather than his

---

[3] Bruce A. Ware, "An Evangelical Reformulation of the Doctrine of the Immutability of God," *JETS* 29, no. 4 (December 1986): 434.

[4] See Bruce A. Ware, *God's Lesser Glory: The Diminished God of Open Theism* (Wheaton, IL: Crossway, 2000); and Bruce A. Ware, *God's Greater Glory: The Exalted God of Scripture* (Wheaton, IL: Crossway, 2004).

otherness, or immanence rather than transcendence. Nonetheless, he presumed the transcendent self-sufficiency and eternal perfection of God:

> God utterly transcends all lesser reality, then, in that he alone exists eternally and of necessity, and his existence encompasses the fullness of all value and perfection entirely within itself. Any and all other existence, goodness, perfection, power, holiness, beauty, or whatever value one might mention is strictly derivative in nature, as coming to be from the eternal God who alone has all such perfection infinitely and intrinsically.[5]

The third theme to recollect from Bruce's career is that in a subsequent controversy, his reevaluation of the doctrine of God included an evaluation of the intra-trinitarian relations through scriptural exegesis. During this well-known debate between complementarian evangelicals, such as Wayne Grudem and John Piper, and egalitarian evangelicals, such as Millard Erickson and Kevin Giles, Bruce promoted certain Scripture passages that he believed required an account.

Among these significant texts were 1 Cor 11:3 and 1 Cor 15:28, both of which affirm a submissive relationship between "the Son," or "Christ," and "God," the Father. This submission cannot be easily restricted to the human Jesus because the latter text specifically refers to the "Son," a title that touches on Christ's eternal nature. The former text refers to the office of Messiah, which touches on both his divine and human natures.[6] Bruce and a colaborer, Grudem, found similar solutions for explaining the eternal Son's subjection to the Father while retaining his equality with the Father. To do so, they adopted the language of "eternal functional subordination" or "eternal relations of authority and submission." The division that Ware and Grudem employed—distinguishing between eternal ontological equality and

---

[5] Ware, *God's Greater Glory*, 49.
[6] Ware, *Father, Son, and Holy Spirit*, 72–85.

eternal functional subordination—appears to have some precedence in modern biblical theology.[7] I am not convinced of the need for this theological division primarily because the *communicatio idiomatum*, the linguistic cross-referencing between the divine and human natures of the one Christ, is a scriptural phenomenon (see John 17:5; Acts 20:28). It is exegetically unnecessary to assign submission to the Son's divine nature.

Three Queries for Ware

However, the distinction between the eternal function of the Son vis-à-vis the Father and the ontology of Christ, which includes the divine nature, raises several important questions. In the first place, Bruce states, "Eternal (ontological) relations of origin and eternal (functional and hypostatic) relations of authority and submission work like hand and glove" (p. 52). Is he stating that the hypostatic or personal relations within God are functional and not ontological? In the subsequent paragraphs, he seems to affirm this interpretation. If so, are we to conclude that the persons of the Father and the Son are merely divine functions or actions? Do the divine persons thereby lack ontological reality? A charitable reading would take my query regarding Bruce's distinction here as pressing his meaning beyond his intent. Therefore, one could respond that his primary concern was to emphasize the

---

[7] Cf. Gordon D. Fee, *The First Epistle to the Corinthians*, New International Commentary on the New Testament (Grand Rapids, MI: Eerdmans, 1987), 155, 505, 760. This is not the venue for exploring the historical provenance of the distinction of "eternal ontological" versus "eternal functional." However, I imagine the "ontology" versus "function" language is borrowed from Kantian-inspired philosophical exegesis, which is willing to speak of divine act but not divine being. However, the coupling of the adjective "eternal" to the "ontology" versus "function" distinction may be a modern evangelical innovation. The benefit of the distinction is that it allows a trinitarian theologian to speak of difference between the Three without sacrificing equality within the One. However, as we shall see, it creates other difficulties.

unity of the ontology with the functionality of God's inner dynamics. If so, then with a nod to Ware's "hand and glove" metaphor as intended not to divide but to unite the persons, we shall move on.

A second question arises regarding Bruce's ruminations about what constitutes eternity. Traditionally, God has been seen as transcendently eternal in his nature. In the classical tradition, at the very least since Augustine's ruminations on Genesis 1–3 in book 11 of his *Confessions*, God is said to reside above and beyond time in an eternal present. God does not change with time; rather, God is eternal. Time is the run of creation and thus comes into existence only with the creative act of the preexistent Creator. As Augustine prayed to God, "In the sublimity of an eternity which is always in the present, you are before all things past and transcend all things future, because they are still to come."[8] God thus actually sees all of time at once—the past, the present, and the future are known to God simultaneously.

However, Bruce does not appear to follow the Augustinian tradition here. Rather, he presents God in such a way that God has both a past and a future within or alongside his eternity. God is said to experience "eternity past" and "eternity future," which are then related to another level of eternity, that which is "absolutely eternal." The first time I read Bruce combining the language of eternity with the language of time, in his book on the persons of the Trinity, I assumed he spoke illustratively, trying to help his reader imagine limitlessness, or immensity, of God from the limited human perspective. However, I may have misunderstood his underlying view of divine ontology at the time. Now, the question arises as to what should be our view of God's relation to eternity.

One critical issue facing evangelical complementarian theologians, therefore, concerns what it means to say that God is eternal. There are two primary options currently available to us: a traditional

---

[8] Augustine, *Confessions* 11.13; cf. Boethius, *The Consolation of Philosophy*, bk. 5.

view and a more modern alternative. On the one hand, there is the received view that God is above and beyond time, as seen in our summation of Augustine. This has been called "eternalism,"[9] and it argues that God is to be understood as transcending time in an inherent "timelessness." God sees all things that occur throughout all time at once. Eternalism notes the difference between the vantage points of God and man, demanding humility on the part of man in his knowledge about God. There is a mystery about God, a divine "incomprehensibility," which constrains human epistemology. Human beings cannot expect to grasp the immensity of God with their created minds, though God can and certainly does reveal certain truths about himself to human beings. Katherin Rogers and Paul Helm have exposited the traditional or eternalist view.[10]

The alternative view of divine eternity, which may be classified as "temporalism," is championed in the work of William Lane Craig, among others.[11] Temporalism points to some of the conceptual problems of eternalism, though it manifestly does so from the perspective of human conceptuality. The temporalist view of divine eternity prefers to picture God as temporally affected by his active relations to creation.[12] The temporalist view is attractive to those who desire a robust doctrine of libertarian free will. However, it suffers from its own

---

[9] Paul Helm, "Eternity," ed. Edward N. Zalta, in *The Stanford Encyclopedia of Philosophy* (Spring 2014), accessed June 30, 2017, https://plato.stanford.edu/archives/spr2014/entries/eternity/.

[10] Katherin Rogers, "The Traditional Doctrine of Divine Simplicity," *Religious Studies* 32 (1996): 165–86; Katherin A. Rogers, *Perfect Being Theology* (Edinburgh: Edinburgh University Press, 2000); Paul Helm, *Eternal God: A Study of God without Time* (Oxford: Oxford University Press, 1988).

[11] William Lane Craig, *Time and Eternity: Exploring God's Relationship to Time* (Wheaton, IL: Crossway, 2001). One may also refer to the contributions of the Oxford professors Richard Swinburne and Anthony Kenney.

[12] William Lane Craig, "The Tensed versus Tenseless Theory of Time: A Watershed for the Conception of Divine Eternity," in *Questions of Time and Tense*, ed. Robin le Poidevin (Oxford: Oxford University Press, 1998), 221–50.

conceptual problems, including how it logically differentiates time from eternity. The second question facing us is, therefore, should we conceive of the eternal God's relation to time in an eternalist or in a temporalist fashion? There is simply not enough space here to provide a detailed answer, but the question must nevertheless be extended if the evangelical community is to discern a way forward.

A third question, intimately related to the previous two in its concern with divine ontology, or the metaphysical description of God, concerns the relations of authority within the perfect God. What does it mean to say that God is perfect in his power and authority? And if Jesus Christ is God, which all four of the participant theologians herein affirm, how does the Son participate in the perfections of God, especially God's lordship? This seems to me to be the critical question facing those evangelical complementarians who are seeking to be explicitly trinitarian in their theology. How can Jesus be Lord yet be subject to the Father's sovereignty? I will offer my own summary answer to this question and hope for other venues to continue the dialogue.

A Proposal Concerning Divine Perfection

God is perfect. The perfection of God is revealed in his eternal attributes, his intra-divine personal relations, and his external relations with his temporal creatures. Ken Oakes provides a working definition of divine perfection: "To speak of the divine perfection is to say that the one triune God is rich, abundant and radiant in and of himself, the pure coincidence of unity and multiplicity, simplicity and plenitude."[13] While not disputing this definition, I will instead craft a biblical summary. Scripture reveals both the perfection of God and God's guidance

---

[13] Ken Oakes, "The Divine Perfections and the Economy: The Atonement," in *Theological Theology: Essays in Honour of John Webster*, ed. R. David Nelson, Darren Sarisky, and Justin Stratis (New York: T&T Clark, 2015), 238.

of creation toward its own perfection. Or, to state it differently, God is perfect in himself, ontologically, and God perfects what he has created, functionally. We might also say perfection is first a *possession* of God and second a *gift* of God.

The Old Testament bears witness to the perfection of God. Perfection is assumed in the first verse of Scripture, for God simply is before creation: "In the beginning God . . ." From this basic datum, the entirety of the Christian doctrine of God, what systematicians refer to as "theology proper," derives. And from this reality of his own being, God acts toward that which is not God: "In the beginning God created the heavens and the earth." Alongside the eternal perfection of God, Scripture affirms the utter difference between Creator and creation. From the perfection of God's being, God acts perfectly toward that which is not God. Elsewhere in the Pentateuch, this is affirmed: "The Rock—his work is perfect" (Deut 32:4).[14] David also defines God as perfect in his actions toward creation: "God—his way is perfect" (2 Sam 22:31; Ps 18:30). Not only that, but God may share his perfection with his creatures: "and [God] makes my way perfect" (Ps 18:32).

The New Testament teaches the perfection of God with regard both to the Father and to the Son. Human beings are called to mimic the perfection of God the Father: "Be perfect (τέλειος), therefore, as your heavenly Father is perfect (τέλειος)" (Matt 5:48). In the Gospel of Matthew, Jesus defines God's work in creation as moving it toward perfection (τέλος may be translated as "goal" or "end"; cf. 24:6, 14; 28:20). Moreover, human moral perfection or personal integrity (τέλειος) is God's way for humanity entering the kingdom of heaven (19:21). Finally, God the Father is the eternal perfection from whom human perfections are derived and toward whom they are being compelled. God stands at the beginning and the end as the origin and goal of perfection. In summary, Matthew teaches, speaking ontologically, that God

---

[14] Unless otherwise noted, all Scripture citations in this chapter are from the Christian Standard Bible (CSB).

is himself perfection, and, speaking functionally, that God is the origin and end of creaturely perfection. God the Father is perfect in himself, and God the Father through the Son calls us toward his perfection.

According to James, all perfection that is in this earth descends to it from God by grace: "Every good and perfect gift is from above, coming down from the Father of lights, who does not change like shifting shadows" (Jas 1:17). James does several things here that are instructive. First, note that God is, as in the Gospel of Matthew, the only source of perfection. The Father is the sole origin of gracious movement toward creation. Second, God's perfection is bound up with his transcendence ("from above") and his immutable eternality ("does not change"). Logically, if God is not his character, yet is defined by his characteristic attributes, then the attributes themselves would be separable from and superior to God. Theologians have coined the term "divine simplicity" to describe how God's being cannot be extricated from his character in this way. God does not possess holiness or love or sovereignty as detachable composites—God *is* love and holiness and power.[15] Third,

---

[15] Note in the following description of traditional simplicity how God's aseity and eternality are integral to the doctrine of divine simplicity. Note also the Creator-creature distinction that must be upheld. "God exists *a se*, absolutely independently of all that is not Himself. Whatever is not God is created by Him. It is certainly correct to characterize Him as wise, powerful, good, etc., but if wisdom, power, goodness and the rest are necessary to God's nature, but not identical to it, then God depends for his existence on other things. But that is impossible. Therefore God does not possess these qualities. He simply *is* omniscience etc. For God essence and existence are the same." Rogers, "Traditional Doctrine of Divine Simplicity," 167. There are a number of recent debates over the viability of divine simplicity. See Steve J. Duby, "Divine Simplicity, Divine Freedom, and the Contingency of Creation: Dogmatic Responses to Some Analytic Questions," *Journal of Reformed Theology* 6, no. 2 (2012): 115–42; and R. T. Mullins, "Simply Impossible: A Case against Divine Simplicity," *Journal of Reformed Theology* 7 (2013): 181–203. The most substantive recent objection to the traditional view offers a weakened simplicity that emphasizes the social nature of the Trinity. Paul R. Hinlicky, *Divine Simplicity: Christ the Crisis of Metaphysics* (Grand Rapids, MI: Baker, 2016).

this unitary set of divine descriptions, to which systematic theologians assign the abstract term "attributes," is never diminished through the Father's relationship to time ("change") or space ("coming down"). God is perfect in himself and in his actions, in his ontological simplicity and in his functional activity.

But perfection does not merely describe the being of the Father. Perfection also describes the being of the Son. As the book of Hebrews says with a rare nominal form,[16] Christ Jesus is the τελειωτήν, or "perfecter," of faith just as he is the ἀρχηγόν, or "pioneer," of faith (Heb 12:2 NIV). The book of Hebrews elsewhere exalts Christ as the perfection of God's works in priesthood (2:10; 7:28), sacrifice (10:14), and sanctuary (9:11), works that mere human beings could never do through obedience to the law (7:28; 9:9). Rather, in the incarnation, death, and resurrection of Jesus Christ, the perfect God has reached down effectively to bring perfection to humanity. It is important here to identify Christ with both the ontological source and the functional agency of perfection, especially since the divine perfection might be compromised in Christological definition.

Hebrews also says Christ Jesus, the "pioneer" (NIV) of our salvation, was made perfect through suffering (2:10), but this does not mean the Son lacked divine perfection in the first place. Since the heretical challenge of Arius, who taught that the Son of God is less than God, based on passages diminishing the perfection of Christ, theologians have learned to reference the "double account" of Athanasius, the leading orthodox opponent of Arius. Athanasius taught that any text that indicates change or composition in Christ refers to his humanity, while any immutable perfection refers to Christ's deity. Recent commentators have often performed such tasks rather subtly and often presumptively, perhaps reflective of modernist disdain for ontological

---

[16] "Τέλος [etc.]," in *New International Dictionary of New Testament Theology and Exegesis*, 2nd ed., ed. Moisés Silva, 5 vols. (Grand Rapids, MI: Zondervan, 2014), 4:473.

discussion. For instance, in his treatment of this passage (Heb 2:10), one leading evangelical commentator first treated the perfecting of Christ from the perspective of Christ's divine nature, then from the perspective of Christ's human nature.[17]

This twofold rule, distinguishing between the two natures of Christ, so as to preserve the eternal perfections of the divine nature of Christ, is necessary. Diminution or advance in a person's nature indicates a lack of perfection, even if there is a movement toward perfection as a result of grace. For Christ Jesus to be God, he must be perfect. If the perfection of his deity is compromised, he is not God. A contrasting pair of syllogisms may help. Positively, it could be said:

1.   If God is eternally perfect, then God does not change.
2.   Moreover, if the Son is God, then the Son does not change.
3.   Therefore, if the power and authority of God is perfect, eternal, and immutable, then the power and authority of the Son of God is also perfect, eternal, and immutable.

Negatively, we may say it this way:

1.   If the power and authority of the Son is said to increase or decrease, then the power and authority of the Son is itself not perfect but imperfect.
2.   Moreover, if the Son's power and authority are imperfect by nature, then the Son is not divine by nature.

---

[17] First, this modern commentator spoke from the divine perspective of God perfecting man: "Man, created by God for his glory, was prevented by sin from attaining that glory until the Son of Man came and opened up by his death a new way by which humanity might reach the goal for which it was made." F. F. Bruce, *The Epistle to the Hebrews*, rev. ed., New International Commentary on the New Testament (Grand Rapids, MI: Eerdmans, 1990), 80. Second, he spoke from the human perspective of man being perfected: "In order to be a perfect high priest, a person must sympathize with those on whose behalf he acts, and he cannot sympathize with them unless he can enter into their experiences and share them for himself," 81.

3.   If the Son is not divine by nature, then the Son does not possess divine power and authority by eternal participation in the nature of God.

4.   Finally, if the Son does not possess divine power and authority by eternal participation in the nature of God, then the Son only has power and authority by temporal grace as a creature.

We must maintain a stark delineation between the eternal perfection of God and the temporal perfecting of creation. The Creator-creature distinction must be upheld, and Christ as eternal God must be placed on the side of Creator, just as Christ as temporal man must be placed on the side of creature.

Therefore, I feel it is necessary to affirm that the Son of God *as God* eternally and perfectly possesses all divine authority and power. Yes, power and authority flow from God to his Son and his Spirit, just as the divine nature flows from the Father to the Son and the Spirit.[18] This eternal sharing of the divine nature between the three persons is what the classical language intends to communicate using "generation" and "procession." Scriptural texts, several of which my evangelical colleague cites, leave us in no doubt that a movement of authority within the Trinity exists. Authority, like the eternal generation of the One, proceeds from the Father to the Son. However, I believe these texts cannot be used to divide the power of God into lesser and greater portions of possession between the persons without compromising the divine nature of the Three.

Moreover, if 1 Cor 11:3 and 15:28 indicate movement of power and authority between the divine persons, there is biblical evidence that authority, or power or rule or kingdom or lordship, adheres to

---

[18] On the thorny question of the relationship between the person of the Father and the divine essence, please see the perceptive proposal of the late Ralph Del Colle, "'Person' and 'Being' in John Zizioulas' Trinitarian Theology: Conversations with Thomas Torrance and Thomas Aquinas," *Scottish Journal of Theology* 54, no. 1 (February 2001): 70–86.

the divine nature. The eschatological display of divine rule will also demonstrate the unified authority of the divine nature: "On that day the Lord will become King over the whole earth—the Lord alone, and his name alone" (Zech 14:9). Zechariah refers to both a movement in authority ("will become King") and an eternally possessed authority ("the Lord alone").[19] Zechariah also focuses on the unity of that possession ("the Lord alone, and his name alone") as well as its universality ("the whole earth"). This passage makes totalizing claims that can be satisfied only by a metaphysical simplicity for the one God as eternal, immutable, and sovereign.

Finally, while the divine persons lead in certain divine works, I would like to affirm that they share fully in all the divine works. For instance, while the Father leads in election, an election attentive to the ministry of the Son, the Son also engages in election (e.g., John 13:18; 15:19). The shared perfection of the Father and the Son and the Spirit[20] provides a theological rule that helps guide our ruminations about the eternal structure of God, with regard to election or authority, or any other divine attribute or work. Prosopological exegesis applied to the persons of the Three should not be used to undermine the indivisible nature and working of the One.

Among the great documents given to modern evangelicals through the early church are the canonical Scriptures. Scripture provides the norm for all theological discourse, and our proposal concerning the perfect lordship of Jesus Christ as the Son of God must be proved thereby. Passed down to us alongside Scripture are also the communal statements of the Fathers that we know as the ecumenical creeds. These creeds do not carry the weight or authority of Scripture, but

---

[19] God's eternal perfection and eternal movement are not incompatible, for his immutability is not static but dynamic.

[20] While not addressed in this essay, I have demonstrated the deity and authority of the Holy Spirit elsewhere. See the summary conclusions in Malcolm B. Yarnell III, "The Person and Work of the Holy Spirit," in *A Theology for the Church*, ed. Daniel Akin, rev. ed. (Nashville, TN: B&H Academic, 2014), 522–27.

they convey the truths hammered out in numerous debates by theologians who read God's Word long before and often better than we do. The creeds include the Apostles' Creed, which calls Jesus Christ "our Lord" and defines his eschatological activity as one of judgment. Meaningfully, the Nicene Creed refers to Jesus as "the Lord" before concluding, "his kingdom will have no end." Finally, the Athanasian Creed asserts that both divine omnipotence and lordship belong to God as One rather than as Three: "not three omnipotents, but one omnipotent" and "not three lords, but one Lord."[21]

Based on the above scriptural exposition of divine perfection, buttressed by these creeds, I can only conclude that there is no "eternal relation of authority and submission" between the Father and the Son if that claim requires us to diminish in any way the fully and eternally perfect possession of authority and power by the perfect Son and the perfect Spirit as well as the perfect Father. While my theology of perfection and the creeds' theology of power may not convince, because admittedly all creaturely theologies lack perfection, the One God the Lord remains nevertheless simply, eternally, and immutably perfect.

---

[21] All three creeds have been newly translated in Malcolm B. Yarnell III, *God the Trinity: Biblical Portraits* (Nashville, TN: B&H Academic, 2016), 240–43.

CHAPTER 6

Response to Bruce A. Ware and Malcolm B. Yarnell III

By Matthew Y. Emerson and Luke Stamps

Introduction

The following response will proceed in three parts, each given in the spirit of Christian charity. First, we will respond to both chapters at once, since they will both receive some of the same commendations and criticisms. Second, we will respond individually to Bruce Ware's chapter, and finally we will respond individually to Malcolm Yarnell's chapter.

Given the critical nature of some of our remarks, we want to make clear from the outset our appreciation for the work of Bruce and Malcolm, our fellow Christian brothers and fellow Southern Baptists. Because of space constraints, these commendations and criticisms will be necessarily brief, but we do not want the terseness of our reply to indicate a lack of gratefulness for the work that has been done. Thus, we offer these responses in the spirit of Christian charity and with the

157

hope that we will all grow together in the knowledge and love of our
Lord Jesus Christ, who rules over all things with the Father and Holy
Spirit, one God forever and ever, Amen.

Response to Both Contributors

Upon reading both chapters from our fellow contributors, we were
grateful to find (as we expected) much to appreciate in their essays. We
also found some areas of disagreement with both chapters. Regarding
the former, we commend both Ware and Yarnell for their insistence on
the ultimate authority of the Bible and the importance of grounding
our doctrine of the Trinity in holy Scripture. As Christians and more
particularly as Southern Baptists, we readily affirm, along with Ware
and Yarnell, that the Bible alone is the ultimate, inerrant authority for
our faith. We therefore want to state unequivocally our shared goal
of seeking a *biblical* articulation of the Trinity as the highest priority.
We also appreciate both Ware's and Yarnell's emphasis on knowing
the triune God in a personal way. Theology is for doxology, and if our
theologizing does not lead to a greater love for God and neighbor,
then we have failed at our task. Beyond these points, we also acknowledge the shared language of trinitarian orthodoxy—one God in three
persons—on which we are all dependent. Each of the contributors to
this volume wishes to articulate a doctrine of the Trinity that is not
only grounded in Scripture but also consistent with the great tradition of Christian reflection on this trinitarian mystery. Even when we
diverge (sometimes quite widely) from our fellow contributors on certain points of historical interpretation, we commend them for showing
regard for this shared heritage.

Without minimizing these important areas of common ground,
we wish to point out a few areas of divergence as well. The most
prominent of these differences concerns how we define the

important trinitarian term "person." We are unsure if Ware would wish to categorize his approach as an example of social trinitarian- ism, and we believe that both he would wish to critique (along with us) certain forms of social trinitarianism (e.g., Moltmann's version). Nevertheless, Ware's essay evinces some social trinitarian tendencies, especially with respect to defining the term "person."

According to social or relational models of the Trinity, the divine persons are conceived of as distinct centers of consciousness and voli- tion, who stand in I-Thou relationships with one another.[1] This appears to be the understanding of "person" that is operative at a number of points in Ware's chapter. A key component in Ware's argument is that the persons of the Trinity are distinct "agents," who possess personally exclusive (even if harmonious) purposes and motives in their distinc- tive actions. This way of framing the activities of the triune persons seems to assume some psycho-volitional distinction between them. When Ware comes to speak of the unity of the divine will, what is tacit becomes more explicit. Though he formally affirms the unity of the divine will, Ware also insists that "in some sense" Scripture distinguishes the will of the Son from the will of the Father (p. 47). Ware speaks of the divine will as the divine nature's "volitional capacity," a kind of shared volitional equipment, as it were (p. 47). But he also speaks of the persons who "access," "exercise," or "make use of" this common volitional capacity in distinct ways (pp. 47–48). This language seems to suggest that the divine persons also possess some volitional equipment behind the shared divine will by which they access it in distinctive ways, though always for the common goal of saving sinners. It seems that for Ware the unity of the divine will is mainly a unity of ultimate purpose

---

[1] For a helpful introduction to the debate between the classical model of the Trinity and social or relational models, see Jason S. Sexton, ed., *Two Views on the Doctrine of the Trinity* (Grand Rapids: Zondervan, 2014).

or intention, not the stronger form of volitional unity to be found in the pro-Nicene tradition.[2]

Yarnell's chapter is largely devoid of any hint of social trinitarianism, although there are a few phrases toward the end of his chapter for which we would suggest modification in order to avoid charges of it completely. For instance, on p. 88 Yarnell states that ". . . relations within God are the basis for the male-female relation and thence all relations within humanity." While we would agree that the relational nature of the triune God is the ultimate basis for the relational nature of human beings, we believe that it goes too far to argue that *relations* within God are like ("the basis for") *relations* (read: relationships) among humanity. To be fair, Yarnell distances his position from one version of social trinitarianism, Grenz's "denotative" and egalitarian model. But we believe that drawing such a close connection between the *sui generis* relations of the Trinity and human gender relationships comes too close to implying that the divine persons constitute distinct centers of consciousness and volition.

While social models of the Trinity provide an interesting contemporary rethinking of the doctrine, they stand in sharp contrast with the classical model that emerged from the fourth century, both in the East and the West.[3] Conceiving of the trinitarian persons as distinct, psycho-volitional agents is a relatively late invention in the history of

---

[2] The evidence for the essential unity of the divine will (i.e., a unity inherent in the divine essence) is voluminous in the pro-Nicene Fathers. See, for example, Gregory of Nyssa, *On Not Three Gods*: "There is no decay existent or conceived in the motion of the divine will from the Father through the Son to the Spirit." See also Athanasius, *Against the Arians*, 3.25.10; Basil of Caesarea, *On the Holy Spirit*, 8.20–21; 18.45; and Gregory of Nyssa, *On the Holy Trinity*.

[3] So we resist any sharp distinction between the Eastern and Western Fathers on this front. Stephen Holmes helpfully summarizes why this inherited distinction is now being challenged. See Stephen Holmes, "Classical Trinity: Evangelical Perspective," in *Two Views on the Doctrine of the Trinity*, ed. Jason S. Sexton (Grand Rapids, MI: Zondervan, 2014), 28–30. For a helpful summary of the (very narrow) differences in emphasis between the East and West, see

trinitarian thought.[4] In the classical model, "person" (Greek, *hyposta-sis*) was defined in terms of the relations of origin, or modes of subsistence, within the one, simple, and ineffable divine nature (Greek, *ousia*). So the Father is unbegotten, the Son is eternally begotten of the Father, and the Spirit eternally proceeds from the Father and the Son. These relations, and these alone, distinguished the persons in the classical model.

Closely related to our concern with social trinitarianism is our reticence to draw direct lines from the Trinity to human gender relations, as we noted above. Setting aside issues related to the Creator/creature distinction and the analogical nature of divine predication, we also resist this close connection between the Trinity and gender because of its equivocation on the term "person." Again, in the classical model of the Trinity, "person" does not connote "personality," and "relation" does not connote "relationship," in the modern sense of these terms. We ought not to posit, then, a straight line between complementarian gender roles and the eternal relations of origin. In sum, we are grateful for Ware's and Yarnell's chapters, and for their insistence on a biblical method. We must part ways with Ware, however, on biblical and historical grounds, with respect to how he defines the term "person."

Response to Bruce Ware

In addition to the preceding remarks, there is still more to say regarding each chapter individually. Because we stand relatively further away

---

Richard Cross, "Two Models of the Trinity?" *Heythrop Journal* 43, no. 2 (July 2002): 275–94.

[4] For an impressive defense of this thesis, see Stephen R. Holmes, *The Quest for the Trinity: The Doctrine of God in Scripture, History, and Modernity* (Downers Grove, IL: InterVarsity, 2012); and Mark Husbands, "The Trinity Is *Not* Our Social Program: Volf, Gregory of Nyssa and Barth," in *Trinitarian Theology for the Church*, ed. Daniel J. Treier and David Lauber (Downers Grove, IL: InterVarsity, 2009), 120–41.

from Ware's position on the Trinity, his essay warrants a somewhat
longer response. Our main concern with Ware's essay is his insistence
that structures of authority and submission characterize the *ad intra*
relations of the Trinity, so, for example, the Father can be said to have
"ontological primacy" over the Son (p. 37). We believe that this position not only is out of step with the great tradition of Christian orthodoxy, but also is inconsistent with a proper understanding of Scripture
itself. Our interaction with his chapter is divided into three categories:
biblical, historical, and theological. Each of these categories raises distinct questions, but as we argued in our chapter, they also form an
integral methodological whole.

Biblical

Regarding the biblical data, we again want to commend Ware for his
insistence on turning to the Bible for theological construction. It is
evident at every turn in his chapter that his primary concern is faithfulness to the Word of God. We are united with him in this respect.
Nevertheless, we take issue with a few points in Ware's treatment of
the biblical material. The first issue concerns a question that we raised
in our chapter: what does it mean to be "biblical"? Ware's approach
seems to be focused mainly on the compilation and exegesis of discrete texts. Without considering the broader contexts of these texts,
this approach runs the risk of proof texting—that is, collating passages
on a given topic and drawing conclusions from the exegetical aggre-
gate.[5] Ware also seems implicitly to pit the plain meaning of Scripture
("using language that reflects what these passages say," p. 27) against
later patristic formulations. But as we argued in our chapter, we find

---

[5] This is not to say that all that has been categorized as "proof texting" is
inappropriate. See, for example, the case made by R. Michael Allen and Scott R.
Swain, "In Defense of Proof-Texting," *JETS* 54, no. 3 (September 2011): 589–606.

this approach hermeneutically and theologically insufficient. Care must be taken to consider not only the literary context of each passage under review, but also its redemptive-historical and canonical contexts, as well as the synthetic theological judgments that emerge from considering the biblical revelation as a whole. Ware does not always show the same concern for these broader horizons of biblical interpretation.

This tendency can be seen, for example, in Ware's listing of texts that purportedly demonstrate the submission of the Son to the Father in eternity future (pp. 31–34). Ware acknowledges that he will not comment on each text, and we certainly understand that the constraints of a single essay prevent an exhaustive study of every passage in all of its contexts. Nevertheless, Ware seems to believe that these passages teach, rather straightforwardly, a submission of the Son to the Father in eternity future which is distinct from his submission in the incarnation. But in the absence of more exegetical and theological argumentation, his list of texts simply begs the question. Far more plausible in our view is that these texts simply extend the Son's *incarnate* submission into eternity, since the incarnation itself is eternal. This future "eternal submission" of the Son is thus a part of his ongoing mediatorial work as the Messiah. It is inappropriate, therefore, to read these texts as straightforward evidence for the *ad intra* submission of the Son to the Father. But even here, this judgment is informed by broader canonical and synthetic considerations and not simply by observations of a single text or group of texts.

Closely related to the issue of context is a second problem we see in Ware's treatment of the biblical material: his failure to attend carefully to what patristic scholars refer to as "partitive exegesis." According to this ancient hermeneutical rule, interpreters must be careful to distinguish between passages that speak of the Son in terms of his divine personhood and passages that speak of the Son in terms of his incarnate mission. An important biblical text in this regard is Phil 2:5–11, which assigns two "forms" to the person of the Son: the form of God and the form of a servant. This passage makes clear that the incarnation is the proper locus in which to understand the Son's servitude and obedience to the Father. The Son, who is by nature equal with the Father, *becomes* obedient. In other words, it is only with a view to the economy of salvation that we can speak of the Son submitting to the Father. So, in our view, all the passages that Ware cites as evidence for the "eternal" submission of the Son to the Father can be explained in terms of the Son's economic mission.[6] Even those passages (such as John 6:38) that speak of the Son as submitting *unto* the incarnation (and not merely *in* the incarnation) should be understood in terms of the economic and contingently willed plan of redemption. And while the economic missions of the Son and Spirit fittingly reflect their immanent processions, not everything that obtains in the missions can be read back, so to speak, into these *ad intra* processions. In our view, it is a category error to speak about "obedience" and "submission" when it comes to the immanent life of the Trinity. The persons of the Trinity share in the one will and authority that inheres in the divine nature. They are only distinguished *ad intra* in terms of the relations of origin.

A third issue arises when we consider Ware's interpretation of certain biblical locutions. Ware tends to read too much into the biblical prepositions regarding the work of the triune God. Ware rightly observes that the Bible consistently speaks of God's actions as proceeding from the Father, through the Son, and by the Spirit. This pattern unquestioningly reflects a certain *taxis*, or order, in the one work of the triune God. But we believe that Ware is wrong to conclude that

---

[6] "Eternal" is an interesting term in this context. There is a sense in which the economy of redemption is "eternal," in that it was eternally (though contingently) willed by the triune God "before" time began (assuming, with the majority Christian tradition, divine atemporality). So the more relevant question is not whether the Son's "obedience" was eternal, but whether it was immanent and not merely economic—or whether his obedience is merely *ad extra* or in some sense *ad intra*.

this order demands what we might call a suborder, or subordination—functional or otherwise—of the Son and Spirit to the Father in their *ad intra* relations. Interestingly, Ware's argument is similar to the one Eunomius and others used in the fourth century to deny the full divinity of the Spirit. Clearly Ware does not want to affirm the Eunomian conclusion, but this line of argumentation—arguing for submission on the basis of the biblical prepositions—was sharply criticized by the pro-Nicene party.[7]

Another example of overinterpretation can be found in Ware's understanding of the divine names. Here Ware attempts to align himself with the tradition, using the divine names not only as an argument for the three persons' shared divinity (a point on which we agree) but also as an argument for gradations of authority between the three persons. Ware argues that the Fatherhood of the Father necessarily implies the "intrinsic paternal hypostatic property of having authority over his Son" (p. 51). Likewise, the Son's generation from the Father necessarily implies his submission. Ware seems to be confusing the way of knowing (human fathers and sons) with the way of being (the divine Father and the divine Son).[8] Father and Son are divinely given names that express who they are in their eternal relations, but the precise analogical overlap with human fathers and sons is not always apparent. Furthermore, the name "Spirit" bears no obvious connection to relations of authority and submission, and yet Ware clearly believes that the Spirit submits to both the Father and the Son. In our view, it is neither required nor prudent to read notions of authority and submission into the divine names "Father," "Son," and "Holy Spirit." Instead, these names simply (though ineffably) communicate the relations of

---

[7] Christopher A. Beeley, *Gregory of Nazianzus on the Trinity and the Knowledge of God: In Your Light We Shall See Light*, Oxford Studies in Historical Theology (New York: Oxford University Press, 2008), 297.

[8] Still, not all human father-son relations imply authority and submission; for example, an adult son who is no longer under the authority of his father and mother.

origin: the Son is eternally generated from the Father and the Spirit is eternally "spirated" (breathed out) from the Father and Son.[9]

Historical

We also have some concerns with Ware's understanding of historical theology and some particular historical sources. On the broadest level, it is our judgment that Ware's understanding of what he calls "eternal relations of authority and submission" (ERAS) represents a novel and significant departure from the historic doctrine of the Trinity. In his essay, Ware suggests three categories for understanding the doctrine of the Trinity: "ontological relations," represented by the eternal relations of origin; "functional relations" of authority and submission that he believes are implied by these ontological relations; and the economic "roles" that the persons assume in redemption. We have some concerns with speaking of the relations of origin in "ontological" terms (they are more properly *hypostatic*), but we are certainly pleased to see that Ware now affirms what he once (at least implicitly) questioned, namely, the eternal relations of origin: the unbegottenness of the Father, the eternal generation of the Son, and the eternal procession of the Holy Spirit. Likewise, we have some questions about Ware's use of the term "roles," but we acknowledge that this category corresponds in some ways with the more traditional "missions" of the Son and Spirit in the economy of redemption. It is the middle category, eternal functional relations of authority and submission, that we find missing in the Christian tradition. Ware himself admits that the theologians of the early church "did not as often" affirm these functional relations

---

[9] On the biblical front more generally, Ware also seems to assume a univocal understanding of divine predication, according to which our language of God can express precisely (though finitely) what God is like in his essence. We see this, for example, in Ware's assumption that sonship demands submission or that the sending requires *ad intra* obedience. We would advocate for an analogical understanding.

(p. 26). We would submit that this category is nowhere to be found in the traditional sources of trinitarian theology.

Even the sources that Ware cites in favor of this position do not demonstrate what Ware wishes to prove. The quotation from Hilary of Poitiers, that the Son is "subject to the Father both in service and in name," need not imply anything more than the eternal procession of the Son from the Father and the submission of the Son in his economic work. Both here and elsewhere in the Christian tradition, theologians have sometimes spoken of the "subordination" of the Son or the "authority" of the Father in these two modes (eternal generation and economic submission), but this language does not demonstrate a "functional submission" that obtains in the *ad intra* relations of the Trinity. Thomas Aquinas, for example, admits that the Father has a kind of "authority" (*auctoritatis*) as the principle of the Son and the Spirit in their eternal relations of origin. But this authority in no way implies subjection (*subiectionem*) or inferiority (*minorationem*) on the part of the Son and Spirit. Aquinas even cites Hilary as an example of this view. [10]

Something similar could be said of Ware's use of Augustine and Jonathan Edwards. As Augustine rightly argues, the Word's sonship did not begin in his economic mission but is instead grounded in his eternal generation from the Father. There is a fittingness to the Son's being *sent from* the Father because the Son is eternally *from* the Father and the Father is not eternally *from* the Son. But, as Keith Johnson has argued elsewhere, this fittingness between the missions and the processions did not imply, for Augustine, an eternal submission of the Son in his eternal procession. [11] The missions reflect the processions

---

[10] Aquinas, *Summa Theologica*, 1.33.1.

[11] Keith E. Johnson, "Trinitarian Agency and the Eternal Subordination of the Son: An Augustinian Perspective," in *The New Evangelical Subordinationism?: Perspectives on the Equality of God the Father and God the Son*, ed. Dennis W. Jowers and H. Wayne House (Eugene, OR: Pickwick, 2012), 125–26.

but cannot be collapsed into the processions. Likewise, the Edwards citation marshaled by Ware simply argues for the "natural decency and fitness" of the missions in light of the processions. Edwards even takes pains to show that the missions are to be distinguished from the processions by virtue of being "established by mutual free agreement." Note as well that Ware's middle category—submission pushed back into the *ad intra* relations—is missing in these citations. This middle category is so problematic because it leads Ware to speak of a gradation of authority within the Godhead in terms of his immanent life, which brings us to some comments of a more dogmatic nature.

Dogmatically

The most problematic language in Ware's essay appears in this context of affirming *ad intra* relations of authority and submission. He speaks of a "primacy" of the Father, not only in terms of his standing as the principle or origin of the other two divine persons (an uncontroversial notion in the Christian tradition), but also in terms of his functional authority over the Son and Spirit. Ware tries to parse this primacy in terms of function rather than ontology (though at one point he also argues for "ontological primacy" [p. 37]), but we are not convinced that this neat separation between function and ontology can be maintained. If the submission of the Son is eternal and necessary, then surely it impinges on what he is (ontology). We resist the idea that "authority" is an exclusively relational term; it is also descriptive of who God is essentially. Furthermore, we are not exactly sure what "functional" relations would even mean when we are speaking of the Godhead *ad intra*. What actions does the one God carry out that require submission and obedience apart from the economy of redemption? Would this imply some kind of potentiality in the inner life of God according to which the divine persons carry out certain functions with regard to one another?

This problem is only exacerbated by the ways in which Ware speaks of the agency of the three divine persons. He is insistent that the Father and the Father alone is responsible for the planning and design of creation and that the Son is merely the agent carrying out a plan that is not per se his own. Ware speaks of plans, motives, and purposes that are "exclusively the Father's" (p. 37). But according to the traditional doctrine of the Trinity, nothing can be predicated of the Father (his unbegottenness and paternity excepted) that cannot also be predicated of the Son and Spirit, on pain of tritheism or else some form of subordinationism. We have already pointed out the social trinitarian tendencies of Ware's proposal, which we believe to have serious consequences for understanding the unity of the Godhead. Ware's attempt to affirm one divine will, even as he posits three distinct appropriations of it (which, as we argued earlier, seems also to require three personal wills), is problematic for affirming the strong monotheism we believe Scripture requires. We remain unconvinced that one can speak of the eternal, *ad intra* submission of one person to another without positing distinct divine wills of some sort. We feel the force of the potential danger of modalism (diminishing the eternal personal distinctions), but we believe that the relations of origin and the *taxis* they imply are sufficient to answer this charge and that to speak of three divine agents carrying out functions that are exclusive to themselves carries its own set of problems.

Conclusion

We wish to urge Professor Ware to reconsider the biblical evidence in light of these interpretive, historical, and dogmatic concerns. We remain convinced that the traditional trinitarian categories—*ousia* and *hypostasis*, properly understood; processions and missions; one divine will and authority—are much to be preferred to the relatively newer categories of functions, roles, and relations of authority and

submission. Relying too heavily on supposedly "plain" readings of
discrete biblical texts, without attending carefully to their canonical
contexts, the history of interpretation, and the dogmatic implications
of our trinitarian categories is simply not an appropriate theological
method in our view.

Response to Malcolm Yarnell

Since Professor Yarnell's essay is indicative of the "middle ground,"
we find ourselves in much more agreement with his essay. We should
reiterate here our appreciation of Yarnell's appeal to Scripture as the
final authority and his clear understanding of theology as, ultimately,
a devotional task. We also want to commend Yarnell for emphasizing
and ably explicating two issues that we only tangentially addressed
in our chapter: the possibility of real talk about God and analogical
language. We feel that these emphases are necessary in theologizing
about God, and we hope they are taken up by readers.

We are also in substantial agreement with Yarnell regarding his
articulation of the classic doctrine of the Trinity, emphasizing both
God's oneness and threeness, and with his appropriation of the
Western tradition, emphasizing the horizontal equality of the three
persons of the one God. There are, however, a number of points in
Yarnell's chapter that gave us pause and require a response. While
these appear relatively minor in comparison to our response to Ware,
we feel that they are nevertheless important as we all seek to grow in
the grace and knowledge of our Lord Jesus Christ. We also want to reiterate that Yarnell chose to emphasize the positive aspects of each side
of the debate, rather than coming to a definitive conclusion on some
of the primary questions of this conversation. So our response should
be taken as a request for clarification as much as it is a critique.

First, we question the prudence of drawing too sharp a distinction between what Yarnell calls devotion-oriented monotheism and

substance-oriented monotheism. Though he acknowledges the usefulness of philosophical categories, Yarnell seems to bifurcate these two
approaches. But the difference between God and his creation, which
fuels devotion, is itself ontological. God is wholly other from his creatures. We come to know the triune God devotionally, to be sure, but
this way of knowing does not preclude further reflections on the "way
of being," that is, speaking of God in terms of his essential uniqueness.

This point was crucial for the pro-Nicenes in articulating their doctrine of the Trinity, and it is crucial for us as well. If we posit too much
ontological overlap, so to speak, between God and his creation, then
we can track into theological speculation rather quickly. For example,
ontologically grounding human marital relationships in the inner-
trinitarian relations runs the risk of anthropomorphizing the latter. If
eternal generation as a relation is comparable to human relationships,
then we are forced into all kinds of problematic statements about it.
The venerable tradition of the *via negativa* leads us to say more of what
eternal generation is not than what it is: it is not physical, since God is
pure spirit; it is not temporal, since God is eternal; it does not produce
a second God, since God is one. Speaking too univocally about the
trinitarian relations vis-à-vis human relationships runs the risk of elid-
ing the crucial distinctions between God and his creation. These problems are not new; the pro-Nicenes picked up on them immediately,
and insisted that the relations of origin, like all divine predication, are
analogical in nature. The essence of God is ineffable, and we can only
speak of him by way of analogy. Given Yarnell's fine section on analogical language, we are surprised that he did not lean more heavily on
this theme in his discussion of human relationships and the way they
correlate to relations in God.

This leads to our second criticism, that Yarnell does not appear
to take a firm position on some of the more pressing debates over the
Trinity within evangelicalism. Given the significance of this cardinal
Christian doctrine, it seems best to stake a decisive claim rather than

merely acknowledge the validity of both sides. Yarnell's chapter was largely descriptive, and even its more constructive portions were not always decisive enough, in our view. At times, Yarnell seems to present his position as a kind of "golden mean" between extremes on both sides. Interestingly, he even presents his own view in the third person as a kind of middle way between Grenz and Swain. Likewise, on the hotly contested issue of the Trinity and gender roles, Yarnell seems to affirm both sides of the contemporary debate without taking a strong stand in either direction. He appears to affirm Swain's caution about connecting gender roles to the Trinity, but he proceeds with his own version of that analogy regardless. He concludes his discussion of the contemporary debate over 1 Corinthians 11 without any evaluative comments of his own (pp. 90–91). We would urge Professor Yarnell to follow his logic regarding analogical language to its natural conclusion: that God's life *ad intra* cannot be compared to human relationships in a univocal way. Any talk of relations within God *ad intra* is necessarily analogical and therefore not immediately transferrable into human experience.

A Final Note on Gender Roles

We did not spend much time on the issue of gender roles in our chapter, so here we should make explicit what is implicit there and in our remarks above. The relationship between a husband and wife is not univocally comparable to the relationship between God the Father and God the Son. We acknowledge that passages like 1 Cor 11:3 connect the doctrine of God to gender roles, but we want to insist that this connection is made between human relationships and the economic missions of the three persons of the one God. The Bible does not ever posit or suggest a straight line between complementarianism and God's life *ad intra*. Rather, the submission of a wife to a husband is comparable to the submission of the Church to Christ (Eph 5:22–32) and to the submission of the *incarnate* Christ to the Father (1 Cor 11:3). Because the economic missions are fitting given the eternal processions, it is not as if there is no connection at all, but the connection that exists is not a direct one. Rather, gender roles mirror or reflect the roles seen in the economic missions. Those missions, in turn, reflect and proceed from the eternal relations of origin. But the latter do not contain any hint of subordination, since, as we have argued, that would be ruinous for trinitarian monotheism.

Conclusion

By Keith S. Whitfield

As we noted in the introduction, the scope of this book is limited. The contributors focus primarily on two features of trinitarian theology: their theological methods for constructing trinitarian doctrine and methodological reflections on whether the triune life of God is a model for relationships between human beings, in particular the complementarian relations between men and women. Considering that the triune God is the subject of the book, we acknowledge that this book does concern itself with the central doctrine of Christianity, and its interactions cast a long shadow over our faith. The discussion here has implications beyond the specifics in the book. As J. I. Packer once noted, "All non-Trinitarian formulations of the Christian message are by biblical standards inadequate and indeed fundamentally false, and will naturally tend to pull Christian lives out of shape."[1]

---

[1] Quoted by Jason Sexton, "Conclusion," in *Two Views on the Doctrine of Trinity*, ed. Jason Sexton (Grand Rapids: Zondervan, 2014), 207. See J. I. Packer, *Concise Theology: A Guide to Historic Christian Beliefs* (Wheaton, IL: Tyndale, 1993), 42.

175

Our Triune Faith

Central to the Christian faith is the knowledge of the one, true, living God, who created a people that they may know him and that he might dwell with them. For this very purpose, he reveals himself to us as the triune God, and to know him truly is to know him as the triune one. God the Father reveals himself to us through the incarnation of his Son. Jesus, as the beloved Son of the Father, came to allow us to participate in the love that he has with his Father by the power of the Spirit.

God reveals himself to his creatures whom he created in his own image. As imagers of God, we are granted the unique capacity to know God. In the garden of Eden before the fall, God revealed himself to Adam as a generous and good provider for his people, as the one who determines what is right and good for his creation, and as the one with a wise and comprehensive plan for the entirety of his creative works. Throughout the Old Testament, God reveals himself to Israel and the nations through his stipulations, promises, acts of judgment, and acts of redemption. In the New Testament, we discover that the revelation given in the former days was only proleptic, and God would reveal himself definitively in the sending of his Son. As John writes, "No one has ever seen God. The one and only Son, who is himself God and is at the Father's side—he has revealed him" (John 1:18). The Bible makes it clear that while God spoke before sending his Son, in the last days, he reveals himself through himself in the sending of his Son, who is "the radiance of God's glory and the exact expression of his nature" (Heb 1:2–3). It is only in knowing God through the Son that we receive God's greatest gift for us: eternal life (John 14:6–7; 17:3). Indeed, throughout the Bible, life is maintained by knowing, worshiping, and obeying God on the basis of who he is (Gen 2:15–17; Rom 8:1–3; and Eph 4:17–18).

Christian salvation is an act of the triune God emerging from God's triune life. Jesus explains the trinitarian shape of salvation in John 17:20–26. Jesus came into a world that had rejected his Father with the mission to show the world the Father's love (vv. 25–26; see John 1:14, 18; 3:16). By the power of his redeeming work, the redeemed are transformed by this love and are called to love as they have been loved (v. 26; see 13:34–35; 1 John 4:8–10). Because the Son comes from the Father, he is uniquely qualified for this task because he has known the Father fully and eternally (v. 25; see John 1:1–3, 18). The New Testament teaches that the redeemed are adopted into God's family and participate in the divine life through union with the Son by the Spirit (John 1:12–13; Eph 1:5–6; 2:5–6; 3:6; Col 2:9–13; 3:3–4; 2 Pet 1:3–4; Heb 2:11).

Models of Trinitarian Theology

Theology studies the nature of the triune God and his acts and how all of reality relates properly to God. With only a few exceptions, the focus of much of twentieth century trinitarian theology has been to demonstrate how God's being, his life *ad intra*, relates to God's acts, his life *ad extra*.[2] In recent studies, theologians have recovered the importance of the divine names—Father, Son, and Spirit—for connecting God's being with God's external activity.[3] Each contributor in

---

[2] There are no doubt exceptions to this rule. In fact, Scott Swain recently demonstrated that B. B. Warfield's treatment of "Father," "Son," and "Spirit" would be such an exception. Warfield in his most mature reflection on the doctrine of the Trinity did not offer a theological accounting for God's acts based on his being because he did not associate personal properties with the divine name. Furthermore, based on Warfield's conclusion, the divine names do not actually reveal the triune God because the divine persons' internal relations do not correspond to the divine names. None of the contributors in this book track in the direction of Warfield's conclusions. Scott R. Swain, "B. B. Warfield and the Biblical Doctrine of the Trinity," *Themelios* 43, no. 1 (2018): 10–24.

[3] See R. Kendall Soulen, *The Divine Names and the Holy Trinity, Volume One: Distinguishing the Voices* (Louisville, KY: Westminster John Knox, 2011); and Scott Swain, "Divine Trinity," in *Christian Dogmatics: Reformed Theology for the Church Catholic*, ed. Michael Allen and Scott Swain (Grand Rapids: Baker, 2016), 78–106.

this book attests that the divine names do in fact reveal the triune God as he is in himself, and that God's external actions correspond in some way to the triune God's inner life. In this section, we intend to summarize how each author accomplishes this task. Before we do so, it is important to note some methodological differences between Ware, Yarnell, and Emerson and Stamps.

The proposals and responses found in this book revolve primarily around one's method for doing trinitarian theology. Theological method is a crucial consideration because it determines both *how* we come to know the object of our studies and *what* we can know about the object of our studies. What questions we ask and how we pursue the answers to the questions are foundational to theological reflection. Theological inquiry, and consequently its method, is a unique subject matter because the object of study is the personal, triune God, who reveals himself to his creation. Thus, we begin by recognizing that he is both knowable by his revelation and the one who knows himself. The good news for us is the triune God wants to be known and reveals himself to us. Before we begin to know him, he already knows us—a truth that Paul so eloquently captures in these words: "Now I know in part, but then I will know fully, as I am fully known" (1 Cor 13:12 CSB).

Each of the contributors privilege the role of Scripture as the primary source for theological enquiry. They unanimously affirm and practice the reformation doctrine *sola Scriptura*. While Scripture is the primary source of our theology, we recognize that the role reason and tradition play in our biblical interpretation remains fundamental to theological projects. In this book the authors have integrated Scripture, reason, and tradition differently. The distinction between their methods significantly determines their respective theological proposals.

For Emerson and Stamps, their biblical judgments are governed by Scripture, "guided by the biblically derived rule of faith, [and] guarded by biblically derived tradition" (pp. 12, 105, 141). Thus, their method does not follow "discrete steps in an irreversible order" (p. 108). Ware does not provide as much meta-reflection on method as Emerson and Stamps give us, and his approach differs discernably from Emerson and Stamps. While he does not ignore tradition, he is not constrained in his judgments by the "guide" of the rule of faith and "guard" of tradition in the same way. Thus, he says,

> I fully agree with the pro-Nicene doctrine of appropriations and find it biblical and right to depict the divine trinitarian operations as expressive of their eternal modes of subsistence. Yet, while what I affirm in this chapter fully accords with this pro-Nicene understanding, I believe that the appeal to divine appropriations falls short of expressing fully what Scripture indicates regarding the functional relations and operations of the trinitarian persons. Yes, the order of operations *ad extra* is expressive of the order of relations *ad intra*, but saying only this excludes a significant portion of scriptural indications. (p. 24)

Yarnell distinguishes himself from Emerson and Stamps in how he relies on tradition, but he demonstrates a more ruled reading of Scripture than Ware. We discover in these proposals how one's method determines "the activity of theological refinement through systematic and philosophical reflection" (language that I borrowed and adapted from Emerson and Stamps's summary of their method) (pp. 98–105). For Emerson and Stamps, this activity clarifies the meaning of concepts, demonstrates how theological understanding is deepened by rightly understanding pro-Nicene doctrines, and explores the implications of the inherited theological grammar. We see, however, from the quote above that Ware is willing to go beyond what he sees as the limits of the pro-Nicene grammar. And, throughout his essay, Yarnell operates cautiously less constrained than Emerson and Stamps and more constrained than Ware by the classic trinitarian grammar.

In addition to acknowledging the methodological differences regarding how tradition rules one's interpretation of Scripture, we also wish to compare how the classical trinitarian language/grammar operates in the respective proposals. By examining the interpretation and function of the trinitarian grammar, one may perceive more clearly the differences and similarities presented here.

Ware argues that the divine persons—Father, Son, and Spirit—are coequal and coeternal based on *equality of identity*, which is his way of affirming that the divine persons possess the same divine nature fully and equally. He also demonstrates that this reflects how they are distinct. First, he says that they are distinct based on *ontological relation*, or their eternal relations of origin. He follows the classic language to distinguish these relations of origin: "unbegotten" for the Father, "eternally begotten" for the Son, and "eternally proceeds" for the Spirit. The relations of origin designate the distinction between the divine persons.

According to Ware, these relations of origin also establish the *functional relations* of the divine persons for the life of God *ad intra* and the life of God *ad extra*. He writes, "These three distinct hypostatic identities, then, are not interchangeable, nor are they true merely of the economic Trinity *ad extra*; rather, they are the eternal unchangeable, fixed hypostatic identities of the persons of the immanent Trinity *ad intra*" (pp. 20–21). On this basis he introduces *functional relations* as another way to distinguish the divine persons. He suggests this revision to the pro-Nicene doctrine because he argues that the doctrine of divine appropriations does not account fully for how Scripture portrays the functional relations and operations of the trinitarian persons. This conclusion follows his interpretation of the divine names. Ware says, "[The Father] acts in a manner that befits who he is as Father" (p. 21); the Father acts as the one with "paternal authority" (p. 23). The Son likewise acts in keeping with what it means to be a Son and assumes the role of submission under the authority of the Father.

Yarnell constructs his essay anticipating the need to address the appropriateness of applying trinitarian theology to human social and relational concerns. At the beginning of his essay, he establishes that whatever importance the Trinity may have for application, theology must precede anthropology. He lays claim to this order by observing two ontological principles from Gen 1:26–27. First, humanity is created by God, and second, humanity reflects God's likeness. Yarnell advances theological realism that reflects trinitarian doctrine of revelation. He concludes, "The divine reality is revealed in and through Jesus Christ. In Christ (and we would add, by the Spirit), there is no gap between divine reality and divine revelation, even if our perception of that reality is corrupted through sin" (p. 73). Yarnell affirms not only that God reveals himself with trinitarian agency, but also that God reveals himself to be triune. He interprets this to mean that divine names signify the "orderly direction in the eternal relations of the person of the Trinity" (p. 80). This affirmation is essentially synonymous with Ware's category of *ontological relations*.

Yarnell follows the Cappadocian fathers in affirming a "vertical" nature in the ordering of the relations among the divine persons. The Father is the "principle or fontal source" (p. 81) of the triune life. This position could suggest the conclusions expressed by Ware's category of *functional relations*, but these insights should not be interpreted as carrying the same meaning. Yarnell connotes no sense of "authority" in the vertical nature of the *taxis*. This formulation merely relays the nature of the order expressed in the doctrines of enteral generation of the Son and eternal procession of Spirit. Yarnell correlates theology and anthropology at the end of his essay, suggesting that based on the doctrine of the *imago Dei*, there is reason to believe the divine life provides a pattern for male-female relations specifically and relations among all of humanity generally. He is, however, cautious in describing the precise nature of that pattern.

With their Spirit-reliant canonical, creedal, and dogmatic method, Emerson and Stamps provide us with a framework for theological reflection. They engage a set of doctrinal coordinates that, in their words, "does not so much solve the mystery of the 'Undivided Light' as it gives us the proper grammar needed in order to speak of it truly and reverentially" (p. 108). The coordinates are: One Nature/Three Persons, One Will/Three Modes of Subsistence, and Inseparable Operations/Appropriation. "One nature" refers to the affirmation that the divine persons share fully in the divine essence. The subsequent references to "one will" and "inseparable operations" reflect the oneness of God in more detail. These qualities of trinitarian grammar are employed in juxtaposition to aspects of the three divine persons. "One divine will" is combined with "modes of subsistence" to annunciate that the divine persons share the same volitional capacity to will as well as the divine desire and plan, and yet they express the divine will specific to their unique relation of origin. In like manner, amid the final pairing of "inseparable operation" with "appropriation," they affirm that the divine persons share the same divine power as they exercise their respective economic functions. A symmetrical pattern exists among the three coordinates. The "oneness" reality of trinitarian doctrine is reflected in the first concept of each of the pairs, and the second concept represents the reality of threeness in trinitarianism. It is through these three sets of coordinates that they provide an interpretation of the divine names: Father, Son, and Spirit.

These paralleled coordinates are not the conclusion of their theological enquiry, but rather are employed by Emerson and Stamps in the process of doctrinal formulation and exposition. This methodological move leads Yarnell to distinguish his reflective process from Emerson and Stamps's in his response chapter. Yarnell observes that Emerson and Stamps are more theologically conditioned by tradition than he is. Yet the coordinates permit Emerson and Stamps to elucidate what they are saying theologically and what they are not saying. It permits them to discuss the profound "mystery of the 'Undivided Light,'" so that one may know (truly) the Triune God. At the same time, the coordinates retain some degree of "conceptual space" between the poles for us "to behold God in reverent mystery."

Three Crucial Questions Remain

The discussion in this book has granted these Baptist theologians an opportunity to work out their trinitarian doctrine in light of the evangelical debate on the eternal functional subordination (EFS) of the Son to the Father. I appreciate the care, clarity, and precision each of the authors used in their contribution to this discussion. As we wrap up this project, I will seek to explain the significance of the three questions at the center of this discussion in order to further the reader's reflection.

What do the Scriptures indicate about the nature of the triune life by the divine names of Father, Son, and Spirit? Yarnell and Emerson and Stamps all follow what Yarnell calls the *connotation model* for interpreting the divine names, which claims that the names "convey the object's nature to some extent" (p. 80). Although he does not describe it as such, Ware appears to follow the *denotation model.* According to Yarnell, this model affirms "that the proper names provide a 'direct reference' to differentiate this subject from all others" (p. 80). This consideration hinges on hermeneutical judgments. Some of these judgments include answering these questions: Should these names be interpreted analogically or univocally? Generally, do we assume an analogy of being so that what we know of the relationship between earthly fathers and sons informs our knowledge of the relationship between heavenly Father and Son? More specifically, to what extent should the familial patterns of the ancient world inform our understanding of the relationship between the Father and the Son? How should the interpretations of the early church theologians condition our reading of these names? And how should the doctrines of eternal generation and procession inform our interpretation of the divine names?

How does the economic mission of the Son and the mission of the Spirit correspond respectively with the eternal generation of the Son and the eternal procession of the Spirit? Previously in this chapter, the issues related to this question were expressed more generally when we suggested that twentieth-century trinitarian theology was focused on demonstrating how God's being, his life *ad intra*, relates to God's acts, his life *ad extra*. The more direct framing of the question helps us appreciate the concern. How does sending correspond with generation and procession? For Ware, the way these realities correspond is most fully conceived by the categories *ontological relations* and *functional relations*. Ware explains what he sees as the necessity of this revision in his response chapter. He writes,

> Do these relations of authority and submission begin, as some insist, only in the incarnation? This just cannot be. It makes a mockery of the Father's sending of the Son, his motive of love, and his purpose to save, that he—the Father—has willed in his Son. It also fails to account for the submission of the Spirit to the Son, where the Spirit is not the subject of some incarnational condescension (John 16:13–14). Well then, does the relation of authority and submission begin in the *pactum salutis*? Certainly, this accounts for the economic Trinity's works *ad extra*, but it does not account for our second question. Why do they begin (if they do so begin) the way they do? (p. 135)

Thus, he concludes that the order of acting is distinct from the covenant of redemption (*pactum salutis*).

Yarnell and Emerson and Stamps argue that generation and procession refer only to relations of origin. However, this affirmation appears to leave us with what some may view as two incommensurate categories—*being* and *act*—that cannot be corresponded. The doctrines of generation and procession establish distinction between the divine persons and provide an order for the relations in the divine life. They do not appear to account for specific activities in the divine economy such as the obedience of the Son to the Father. Yarnell does not address this problem in his essay. Emerson and Stamps, however, implicitly demonstrate that the doctrines of generation and procession and the doctrine of the divine mission may not be as disproportionate as some might conclude. They do this by pairing the doctrine of inseparable operation with the doctrine of appropriation. In this pairing, they account for how the manner of divine acts in creation, providence, and salvation corresponds with the manner of God's being. In this move, the doctrines of generation and procession are not left to carry the burden alone for establishing the correspondence between act and being.[4] So does Ware's supplementing of eternal generation with *functional relations* best describe the extension of the divine eternal relations in the economy theologically and best reflect the biblical teaching? Or do Emerson and Stamps's paired coordinates do all the work that is necessary to show how the triune God's modes of being correspond with his modes of acting?

How can the three divine persons act and relate to one another if there is only one divine will? And more specifically, how is the "willing" of the Son best accounted for? Emerson and Stamps argue that will is a capacity of the divine nature and that conception of the will entails "volitional *faculty*, not merely a shared desire, plan, or intention" (p. 119). Thus, the three divine modes of subsistence relate to each other according

---

[4] Keith Johnson has recently demonstrated that Augustine's trinitarianism accounts for the correspondence in a similar way. See Keith E. Johnson, "Trinitarian Agency and the Eternal Subordination of the Son: An Augustinian Perspective," *Themelios* 36, no. 1 (2011): 7–25. For a discussion on the way Karl Barth accounts for the correspondence, see also Scott Swain and Michael Allen, "The Obedience of the Son," *International Journal of Systematic Theology* 15, no. 2 (2013): 114–34.

to their relation of origin, and these relations do not have distinct "volitional equipment" (p. 123). They follow recent expositions of the covenant of redemption to sustain both their pairing of "one divine will" and "three modes of subsistence." They explain, "Both Owen and à Brakel affirm the singularity of the divine will, but also speak about 'distinct applications' of (Owen) or distinct 'perspective[s]' on (à Brakel) this one divine will, corresponding to the distinct modes of subsistence in it" (p. 124). Following this explanation, they quote Swain's reference to the "will's unity and indivisibility" and the "will's tripersonal manner of subsistence"[5] (p. 124).

In their response to Ware's essay, Emerson and Stamps raise concerns about how he addresses the unity of the divine will. They suggest Ware's "framing [of] the activities of the triune persons seems to assume some psycho-volitional distinction between them" (p. 159). Further, they argue,

> Though he formally affirms the unity of the divine will, Ware also insists that "in some sense" Scripture distinguishes the will of the Son from the will of the Father. Ware speaks of the divine will as the divine nature's "volitional capacity," a kind of shared volitional equipment, as it were. But he also speaks of the persons who "access," "exercise" or "make use of" this common volitional capacity in distinct ways. This language seems to suggest that the divine persons also possess some volitional equipment behind the shared divine will by which they access it in distinctive ways, though always for the common goal of saving sinners. (p. 159)

Ware anticipates this objection, and he seeks to clarify his position in the final paragraph of his response chapter. He refers to his previous

---

[5] Scott R. Swain, "Covenant of Redemption," in *Christian Dogmatics: Reformed Theology for the Church Catholic*, ed. Michael Allen and Scott Swain (Grand Rapids: Baker, 2016), 117–18.

affirmation for a unity of will, and also appeals here for the need to distinguish "hypostatic willing(s)" (p. 137). In establishing this point, he appeals to Emerson and Stamps's affirmation of Owen and à Brakel, and he concludes,

> Each trinitarian person wills the one will but in distinctive ways. . . . There is one and only one will in God in terms of volitional capacity of the nature of God and in terms of the content of that will. Yet there must be hypostatically distinct expressions of that will . . . So the content of the willing of each may be in full agreement and expressive of the same fundamental reality, yet the perspective and hypostatic distinctiveness must also be maintained. (pp. 136–137)

Ware suspects there is more consensus between his view and Emerson and Stamps's position than what Emerson and Stamps suggest. Conceptually there are similarities, but the material difference lies in how their affirmations are situated with respect to the covenant of redemption. For Ware, the hypostatic willing(s) reflect the *taxis* in the relation of origin, and for Emerson and Stamps, the "distinct applications" of the divine will by distinct modes of subsistence is grounded in the *pactum salutis*.

Conclusion

There remains more work to be done on the issues raised in this volume. Yet, as we conclude this volume, I return to express again my appreciation for the work of the contributors. I have been enriched by their friendship as well as their biblical and theological reflection through this project. We do this work to know God and to serve the church as she seeks to rightly think about her God. These activities, I believe, reflect the desires of Jesus, which he expressed in a prayer to his Father on the road to Gethsemane. As he lifted his eyes to heaven, he prayed that the divine life would shape our lives. He asks, "that they may all be one, just as you, Father, are in me, and I in you, that they also may be in us" (John 17:21 ESV). This oneness results from the knowledge of the Father through the Son. It is a knowledge that comes to us by his Word (17:6–8, 17), and it provides for us eternal life (17:3). As we seek to know him rightly together, may the Spirit-empowered revelation of Father through Son make us one.

NAME INDEX

SUBJECT INDEX

SCRIPTURE INDEX